W9-BFO-770

TEXAS LAND ETHICS

TEXAS LAND ETHICS

By Pete A. Y. Gunter and Max Oelschlaeger

Photographs by Sharon Stewart

University of Texas Press 🐂 Austin

Copyright © 1997 by the University of Texas Press
All rights reserved
Printed in the United States of America
First edition, 1997

Requests for permission to reproduce material from this work should be
sent to Permissions, University of Texas Press, Box 7819, Austin, TX
78713-7819.

∞ The paper used in this publication meets the minimum requirements
of American National Standard for Information Sciences—Permanence
of Paper for Printed Library Materials, ANSI Z39.48-1984.

Library of Congress Cataloging-in-Publication Data
Gunter, P. A. Y. (Pete Addison Y.), 1936–
    Texas land ethics / by Pete A. Y. Gunter and Max Oelschlaeger. —1st ed.
        p.   cm.
    Includes bibliographical references (p.   ) and index.
    ISBN 0-292-72802-6 (alk. paper)
    1. Environmental ethics—Texas.   2. Environmental responsibility—
Texas.   3. Environmental policy—Texas.   I. Oelschlaeger, Max.   II. Title.
GE42.G86   1997   96-51314
363.7'009764—dc21

CONTENTS

Acknowledgments — vii

Introduction — ix

1 What Is a Land Ethic? — 1

2 Texas: The Land and Its Communities of Life — 19

3 Texas: A State of Neglect — 31

4 Land Ethics and Economics — 63

5 Are Land Ethics Practical? — 81

6 The Big Thicket — 107

7 A Conclusion — 129

Bibliography — 139

Index — 145

ACKNOWLEDGMENTS

We would like to thank Bernie Schermetzler of the Aldo Leopold Archives at the University of Wisconsin–Madison for his help in running down copies of the letters Leopold wrote while in the Big Thicket. Champion International and Temple-Inland corporations are due our thanks for their help in understanding their present and planned future policies in East Texas. Gratitude is due, similarly, to the Texas Parks and Wildlife Department and The Nature Conservancy for bringing us up to date on their holdings in the Big Thicket.

About the Photographs

The photographs for *Texas Land Ethics* are from the critically acclaimed exhibition and photonarrative, *Toxic Tour of Texas*, by Sharon Stewart. Since 1992, the exhibition has been seen in libraries, civic centers, and museums throughout Texas under the joint sponsorship of the Texas Humanities Resource Center and the Texas Photographic Society.

INTRODUCTION

Texas has been and in some ways still is a frontier society, though the frontier ended in the early 1900s. Somehow the frontier mentality, the notion that nature's bounty is unlimited, virtually free for the taking, must be put behind as we enter the twenty-first century. This myth configures itself in many ways, such as in the belief that new resources will always be found to meet the expanding demands of a physically growing, materialistic society.

The frontier mythology also lingers on in the belief that economy and ecology, or jobs and the environment, are at odds. Even if this idea were true, which it is not, Texans would lose out in the long run: devastated environments have invariably ruined the societies that depended on them, most tellingly by destroying their economies.

Like it or not, this generation faces a challenge every bit as real as did the frontiering people who first inhabited the state. Their challenge was physical survival, making an often recalcitrant land yield a living. Ours is sustainability, the building of a way of life that draws from the land without degrading it or impairing basic ecological processes. Can we shape a sustainable tomorrow? A tomorrow where economics and ecology have somehow been reconciled, and where Texans have some rational expectation that their daughters and sons and future generations might prosper, yet live in environments free of pollutants and scars, where some wild lands still exist and animals range freely? Such are the questions we explore here.

As Texas nears the twenty-first century, a few citizens are beginning to favor a different way of thinking about the interrelations of nature and culture, one that helps them to perceive the relation as less oppositional than cooperative. *Texas Land Ethics* is a small contribution to that effort. In this regard we are optimistic: we believe that men and women of good will who have shared interests, whatever their differences, can forge an ecologically sane and economically viable tomorrow.

In another way we are less optimistic. Our considered opinion is that if Texans, as we will try to make clear, continue to live in the mythology of the past, then at some point, perhaps within the next two or three decades, the die will have been cast. It will be too late. Our argument is rooted in almost overwhelming evidence that Texas has gone well past the point where it could continue with business as usual. When it comes to the land, Texas is a state of neglect. Consider just a few relevant facts.

．　．　．

Since World War II, the population of Texas has increased by more than 10 million. We will likely gain another 7 to 10 million in the next twenty years. Thus Texas will have an estimated 22 million people by the year 2010, most of them located in the so-called Texas triangle, with the Dallas–Fort Worth metroplex at the top and Houston and San Antonio at the base. Ironically, one reason for our meteoric population growth has been the quality of life in the Sunbelt. Yet as the human population expands, the quality of life declines. Roads become increasingly crowded, property taxes rise to build the infrastructure necessary to sustain urban growth, and pollution fouls air and water.

More than half of all Texans breathe air that does not meet present quality standards. And more than 5,600 violations of the Safe Drinking Water Act occurred in Texas from 1989 through 1991. Texas ranks thirty-eighth nationally in spending on water-quality protection programs (approximately $3.7 million/year compared to the national average of $33.5 million). Texas also ranks near the bottom among states on overall spending for environmental programs as a percentage of total budget (0.6 percent compared to the national average of 1.89 percent). And we lead the nation in emission of greenhouse gases (whose function we will explain later). Our yearly per capita average is 27.26 tons of greenhouse gas (measured in terms of CO_2 equivalent). For comparison, consider that California, another industrialized, geographically vast state that, like Texas, is heavily dependent on private transportation, has a per capita average of only 15.65 tons per year.

Of course, some actions have been taken to address past environmental mistakes. One is CERCLA, the Superfund law. But cleaning up the toxic messes left behind by corporations is a very expensive business. The Environmental Protection Agency estimates costs of between $420 and $450 million to clean up the thirty Texas Superfund sites. That's only the tip of the iceberg. Compliance with environmental laws—and these laws address only the worst problems—is precipitating a budgetary crisis in city government. Property owners in most Texas cities are going to be forced to foot the bill for environmental protection and cleanup, more often than not for problems they did not create. And the "unfunded mandates" of the 104th Congress imply that either local taxpayers are going to have to dig deep in their pockets to safeguard environmental quality or that large parts of the Texas landscape will come more and more to resemble the ecologically devastated environments of Eastern Europe.

Finally, we must recognize that population growth does not just adversely affect people. The Texas list of "species in trouble" (waiting for placement on the U.S. endangered species list) includes 67 species of birds, 48 of mammals, 38 of fishes, 32 of reptiles, 24 of mollusks, 18 of amphibians, 15 of crustaceans, 6 of insects, and 4 of arachnids. Plants at risk are found in 142 of our 254 counties—76 species in Big Bend National Park alone.

■　■　■

As our story unfolds, we look at some of the root causes which have led to the state of neglect. Our primary concern, however, is not so much with assigning blame, so that good guys in white hats can be distinguished from the bad guys who are despoiling the earth. (When it comes to ecology, there are few if any saints. All of us, including the authors, are culpable.) The issue is simply to begin changing things, the way we live and work, manage our land, secure our food, transport ourselves, build our houses, and so on. We make no claim to occupy the moral high ground, pronouncing judgment on ordinary citizens and commercial enterprises. Instead, as the title of our book suggests, we offer a different way of thinking about the "hard facts" outlined above and of designing appropriate responses, an ecological way of thinking. We are convinced that if enough of us came to perceive the world and our relations to it through a land ethics frame, then sustainability would be within reach. We could live lives of freedom, avoiding the ruin of our environment without destroying our economy.

We are well aware that the very idea of Texas land ethics will be labeled by many as radical, utopian. In truth, whatever labels are assigned, *our claims are conservative* in the truest sense of the word. Texas land ethics do not presuppose the overthrow of either democratic government or a market economy. Our hope is that the practice of land ethics will lead to the renewal of the democratic process and a truly free enterprise system, one that provides meaningful work without destroying the ecological basis of economic life. No doubt we offer analyses and make claims that are critical of some present public policies. We also criticize certain kinds of business practices and commercial enterprises. Big government and big business are part of the state of neglect. But the idea of Texas land ethics recognizes that government and business—and the public—are also part of any realistic discussion of solutions.

The Lay of the Land

As students of Texas history know, our state has been built on abundant natural resources. At one time the land, air, and water appeared to be nearly inexhaustible, capable of sustaining the Texas economy and citizens indefinitely. Texas seemed infinite; the scale of human activities seemed finite. The frontier always beckoned, just beyond the next horizon. Today that perception is changing: Texas is neither so vast nor so infinitely resilient to human insult as we have imagined.

The land crisis to which we refer is usually termed an "environmental crisis." Yet that phrase is problematic. One reason is that it connotes mainstream environmentalism and its agenda, an agenda that is largely anthropocentric, driven primarily by considerations of efficiency and human health. The notion of a "land crisis" has a broader sweep. It involves, in addition to human health and efficiency, considerations like the ecological footprint of human populations, ecological integrity, and the beauty of the land. What is the carrying capacity, in terms of population, of the state of Texas? How many people living for how long could continue to live like the present generation? What are the implications of human population growth for the rest of the land community, assessed in terms of habitat modification, water utilization, and biodiversity?

In comparison to the term "land crisis," "environmental crisis" is remote, abstract, and perhaps too scientific—devoid of any sense of people who are involved with Texas places. Many Texans have had a lifelong love affair with the land: its forms and features, its flora and fauna. Texas litterateurs and poets, ballad singers and historians, painters and photographers have celebrated the land in all its diversity and beauty. The land is something that often brings to mind a specific location, perhaps a mysterious place associated with childhood memories, a beautiful spot visited on a vacation or hunting trip, a familiar family homestead. Regrettably, as Texas has become increasingly urban and industrial, too many Texans have learned to ignore the land; even more abuse it.

Finally, the term "environment," in a *technical sense*, refers only to abiotic, that is, nonliving, aspects of the landscape; the biota, the plants and animals, are not involved. Talk about land ethics, however odd this may seem on the surface, involves the idea of a land community *in which human beings are members*. The very idea of a land community brings to mind something that is social, interactive, and cooperative. In contrast, environment connotes a material entity: passive, inert, even dead.

We will make our case for the validity of this way of looking at things in seven installments. The first chapter goes into the specifics of Texas land ethics, beginning with the vision of the ecologist Aldo Leopold. Originally a mainstream utilitarian conservationist, whose guiding credo was to extract the last measure of economic value from the earth in the most efficient way possible, he ended his career as a proponent of an alternative orientation to business as usual. How is it, he wondered, that human beings can live on the land without spoiling it? His experience in the American Southwest and Midwest as a game manager and forester forced Leopold to answer this question in an unexpected way. In order to treat land effectively, he concluded, it is not sufficient to discover through the joint efforts of science and common sense that we are abusing it. We need an ethic through which we can both value the land and extend to it the ethical concerns that we have used, and broadened, in the past. The three fundamental features which, on Leopold's terms, we are obligated to sustain are: integrity, stability, and beauty. We discuss these in terms of their meanings and in terms of how they relate to each other.

Chapter 2 surveys the Texas landscape itself. Three factors seem to us to describe this landscape: diversity, frontier, and limits. Diversity is evident to anyone who has traveled the state, though often not to outsiders, whose image is often formed by movies and TV. Brownsville is as far south as Miami, Florida. Dalhart, 800 miles due north, has, by contrast, the climate of eastern Colorado. It is not uncommon in winter for Brownsville to bask in 80°F sunlight while Dalhart is hit by snow and biting winds. West to east the contrasts are equally dramatic. Southeast of El Paso the Chihuahua desert garners 8 inches of rain per year while Orange, far to the east, averages 56 inches: parched desert at one extreme, deep forest and cypress swamp at the other. Between the four points of the compass the land varies endlessly. No two of the state's eight major regions have the same resources or the same problems.

Traditionally all of Texas' diversity has fallen under a single heading: Frontier. As long as any American state (nearly a century), Texas was a land frontier, offering new soil to plow, trees to cut, prairies to ranch. When the land frontier ran out around the turn of the twentieth century, the state discovered a windfall in oil and natural gas, and underground water, and entered into a resource frontier. These frontiers are in the past. The present reality is one of limits. As sprawling urban areas ("Slurbs") stretch across the eastern half of the Lone Star State, underground waters dwindle in the Panhandle. As rivers are dammed to provide water for the Slurbs, estuaries and barrier islands are threatened along the Gulf Coast. All this challenges an inherited frontier mentality which promises endless rewards without prior caution, which decrees that serious problems of depletion and pollution cannot exist, and which breathes an aura of anti-intellectualism.

Chapter 3 offers more details concerning the problems that constitute the Texas land crisis. There we offer a broad survey of the "state of neglect" while also paying attention to bioregional problems, such as the overdraft of groundwater that is exhausting the Ogallala Aquifer and the toxics that pollute Lavaca and Galveston bays. Our overview is organized under six headings: population growth, habitat modification, biodiversity, air, water, and waste. While facts that detail the land crisis are important, we are also concerned to show how the land communities that existed historically have been dramatically changed, and with assessing the near- and long-term ecological and social implications of those changes.

Chapters 4 and 5 at first move away from issues of water, species, regions, and waste. They are, directly or indirectly, about economics. We believe that a discussion of economic issues is inescapable, however, if land ethics are to have a chance of being understood. Land and economy, economics and ecology are profoundly interrelated subjects. In interrelating them we will try not to become too abstract, or too far removed from the texture and the landscapes of the Lone Star State. A certain amount of theory is inescapable. But we will attempt to escape it by relating our skirmishes with mainstream economics to specific issues, and places, in Texas.

Chapter 4, on land ethics and economics, discusses the possibility of incorporating land ethics into public policy making and commerce in ways that lead toward sustainability (as distinct from sustainable development). Today we know that the so-called Environmental Impact Hypothesis is incorrect and that a healthy and sustainable economy cannot be built on a faulty ecology. And we know that state economies built—like our own—

on the extraction of resources are doubly challenged. The idea of land ethics does not imply a revolution in our political economy. Texas land ethics must largely occur within the existing institutional structure. There is little chance that Texans can forestall and perhaps avert the land crisis unless we begin now, within the framework that already exists. Markets can be adjusted to reflect the true costs—the ecological and social costs—of doing business. And the good news is, as a number of studies have shown, that although ecological economics will change things, it does not portend economic ruin.

Chapter 5 considers the practical issues, primarily questions concerning the institutionalization of Texas land ethics. Clearly, land ethics would change things. Just as clearly they do not presuppose utopia, but rather ecologically informed and ethically leavened transformation of business as usual. We make two specific suggestions for implementing land ethics: getting the price right and land-use planning. A book of this length cannot hope for comprehensive coverage across the broad array of issues affected by land ethics. Our aim is simply to illustrate how land ethics relate to making public policy, public policy that is not radically utopian, but practical, in both an ecological and a social sense. A citizenry guided by the land ethic avoids either extreme of "locking the land up in perpetuity" (although it protects unique ecosystems from development) or "using it all now." We favor a sustainable approach.

Chapter 6 is a case study in land ethics, focusing on the Big Thicket. The Big Thicket is arguably among the most important examples of ecologically inspired conservation in the United States. Stretching across hundreds of thousands of acres of Southeast Texas from Conroe, on what is now Interstate 45, to the Louisiana border, the Big Thicket has been celebrated as one of the biologically richest and most diverse areas in North America. Tupelo swamps, bears, orchids, roadrunners, alligators, champion trees: the list of its life forms seems endless, as the catalogue of its plant growth associations seems remarkable. Events have not dealt well with this cornucopia, however. Lumber company cutting and oil field destruction have reduced the old wilderness to a fragment of its former self, and recent clearcutting has threatened to destroy its very identity.

In the face of this onslaught conservationists have struggled to preserve at least some minor portions of the original land in its original condition. Their efforts have resulted in a curious and unexpected situation. The creation of state parks, a national biological preserve, corporate donations, a national wildlife refuge, and an apparent shift in lumber company attitudes toward clearcutting open up the possibility that interlocking portions of wilderness might be sustained into the foreseeable future: sustained without depleting the region's economy. This situation is still only a possibility, which might be lost. It is a possibility, however, which only a generation ago appeared impossible.

Finally, the concluding chapter explores the prospects for Texas tomorrow, attempting to avoid either utopian or dystopian claims which are characteristic of, on the one hand, the frontier mentality and, on the other, doomsday environmentalism. Our argument is that enlightened citizens, committed to place, might be guided by the land ethic in building the new Texas. In any case, today's citizens will either respond or suffer the consequences. The state of neglect will not spontaneously ameliorate. We either build the new Texas or face increasingly severe and costly environmental consequences.

TEXAS LAND ETHICS

*Concerned Citizens
against Pollution at Texas
State Capitol, Austin.*

WHAT IS A LAND ETHIC?

Historic Roots: Aldo Leopold

The land ethic concept was created by Aldo Leopold (1887–1948). All attempts to develop or apply such an ethic—including this book—are indebted to his ideas. Though he wrote widely, Leopold's major work is *A Sand County Almanac*. The fruit of long experience and profound reflection, this book unites a deep understanding of nature with profound insights into the human response—and obligation—to it. Any person seriously interested in land, water, biota, and their equilibria could profit from reading it.

Most of us, when we hear words like "biota," "equilibria," and "ethic," tend to think of cloistered intellectuals: or, to use Tom Lehrer's phrase, ivy-covered professors in ivy-covered halls. But this is precisely not true of Leopold. Far from being an ivory-tower speculator, he developed his ideas in the field, as a forester and later as a game manager. Equally impressive from this vantage point is the transformation he underwent. The young Leopold began with the confidence of a lifelong hunter who believed—following elementary arithmetic—that extermination of predators like wolves and panthers would lead to an unlimited supply of deer and other game animals. Similarly, when he started work in the newly minted U.S.

Forest Service, he had every confidence that industrial methods, applied to American forests, would produce an unending stream of lumber without harm to soils, streams, or nontimber species. This viewpoint was extraordinarily hopeful, and it had the virtue of simplicity. But it proved inadequate. Leopold was driven by the sheer weight of his experience to the realization that only a combination of personal responsibility, scientific knowledge, and hard-won wisdom can sustain the land, the forests, and the people who inhabit them. Not just technology, not just economics, but a new "ethic" is necessary.

. . .

Rand Aldo Leopold, the son of German immigrants, was born in Burlington, Iowa, on January 11, 1887. Raised in a big house on limestone bluffs overlooking the Mississippi River, he was nurtured by both a love of learning and a passion for the countryside: a passion which expressed itself first in hunting and fishing, second through knowledge of plants, animals, and their scientific names. Like many prosperous Midwesterners, the Leopolds sent their children east to complete their education. Aldo was to study at Lawrenceville Prep, near Princeton, and then at Yale University's Sheffield Scientific School, where his interests began to point toward forestry. In 1906 he entered the Yale Forest School—the only school of forestry then in the United States.

The rationale of the Yale Forest School—established through gifts of the Pinchot family—was largely provided by Gifford Pinchot, close friend of Theodore Roosevelt and the first head of Roosevelt's U.S. Forest Service. The young Yale Forest School was therefore not merely an institution—it was the spearhead of an entire conservationist movement. It is interesting to examine briefly the nature of this movement, whose inspiration Leopold and his contemporaries at the Forest School shared.

American turn-of-the-century environmentalism—now termed Resource Conservation Ecology—was flatly and unashamedly anthropocentric. That is, it proclaimed that nature exists solely for the good of humankind. In the hands of Roosevelt and Pinchot, its most effective advocates, it spoke in highly nationalistic terms. America's lands, waters, and resources, they proclaimed, exist for the good of the American people; they should be made to produce the "greatest good for the greatest number" for the greatest length of time. Many contemporary conservationists would question this rationale (which its proponents termed "The Doctrine of Highest Use"). They would argue that it is unwise—not to speak of unjust—to conceive humankind as the only creature of value on this planet and all the other living things mere "standing reserve" for human use. They would also argue that Resource Conservation Ecology chose a poor measure of value: economic advantage, usually in the short run. Is it really enough, they would protest, to know the price of everything, but know the value of nothing?

In retrospect the purely economic approach of Resource Conservation seems understandable. Not only does it express the preoccupations of a frontier nation for centuries deeply involved in developing its resources; it expresses also the nineteenth century's faith that the market will always, by itself and without interference, produce the best of all possible economies in the best of all possible worlds. There was a certain irony in this. Operating on these principles the United States had by the turn of the century exhausted its land frontier. Still more ominously, through the old, tried and true "cut and get out" policies of the lumber companies, it was on the verge of exhausting its once abundant timber. The seriousness of the situation was twofold. The country faced the loss of a raw material necessary to home- and shipbuilding and other construction needs. But there was also a danger to its water supplies. Hills and mountains scalped of their brush and timber quickly erode, silting streams, muddying waters. It does not take a subtle mind to see that clean water is necessary not only to public health but to industry and industrial expansion. And the United States was entering into a period of unparalleled industrial growth.

This sticky situation explains why Roosevelt, Pinchot, and their allies moved so quickly to create a system of national forests. Their goal was to protect and sustain the nation's remaining timber (and water) resources by protecting forests, which private lumber companies would otherwise quickly deplete. Their second goal was to manage these forests "scientifically," thus setting an example for the private sector to follow on its own lands. If one liked, this was government interference. But its goal was to reform, not to replace, the timber industry. In any case, action was required, and the Progressive Republicans knew how to get things done.

The young Leopold is often portrayed as a passionate follower of Pinchot and Roosevelt. This was not the case, however, in any simple way. Essentially an individualist, he was temperamentally unable to be an unquestioning disciple. It was understandable, however, given his own background and the pressing needs which Roosevelt's and Pinchot's policies attempted to meet, that he would begin his career with a general belief in their ideas.

In 1909 Leopold joined the U.S. Forest Service (established 1905) and took his first assignment, in District Three, in the Arizona and New Mexico territories. His job was as a field assistant in the Apache National Forest in Southeast Arizona. Though Leopold's experience had scarcely prepared him for the new country, he managed quickly to adapt to it. A year later he was transferred to the Carson National Forest in northern New Mexico, first as deputy supervisor, then as head supervisor. At the age of twenty-five he found himself in charge of a million-acre forest supporting 200,000 sheep, 7,000 head of cattle, 600 homesteads, and a billion board feet of timber.

The young man—who had by then married the daughter of an old and powerful New Mexico Hispanic family—found many difficulties to overcome. His subordinates did not always see eye to eye with this brash young "Easterner," who was often compelled to invent policy on the spot, and who was as capable of miscalculating as any other forest manager. In the end, however, he proved equal to the task. Not only did he become an increasingly important figure in the Forest Service; he became an increasingly active and influential public figure in the Southwest, founding numerous game associations, successfully arguing for the creation of the first wilderness preserve in a national forest (the Gila Wilderness), urging statewide restrictions on the hunting of game animals. He was both an effective advocate of improved watershed management and a stalwart leader in the effort to exterminate deer-eating predators.

On this latter point he certainly showed no lack of single-mindedness. Measures intended to increase game populations, he argued, would produce a specific number of new hunters per number of new deer, which at x dollars per hunter would amount to x-plus dollars of additional revenue per county per year. To increase the number of huntable deer, he continued, it would be necessary to offer a bounty on the "varmints" (wolves, bears, panthers) that eat huntable game. The arithmetic seemed incontestable, unanswerable. Teddy Roosevelt could not have pursued a goal with more vigor.

Looking back on this project and its underlying assumptions, he was to have ample reason to reconsider. In a passage written many years later he describes killing a mother wolf and her yearling cubs on White Mountain, Arizona, shortly after his arrival in the Southwest:

> We reached the wolf in time to watch a fierce green fire dying in her eyes. I realized then, and I have known ever since, that there was something new to me in those eyes—something known only to her and the mountain. I was young then, and full of trigger-itch; I thought that because fewer wolves meant more deer, that no wolves would mean a hunters' paradise. But after seeing the green fire die, I sensed that neither the wolf nor the mountain agreed with such a view. (Leopold 1986)

In fact, it took Leopold many years to discover what the wolf and the mountain knew. At first things seemed to go well. Predators were killed; deer herds increased; hunters applauded. The south-facing slopes of the mountains, however, began to become interlaced with new deer trails. Available bushes and seedlings were browsed into anemic health and finally to death by hungry deer. Edible trees were then stripped of leaves "to the height of a saddle horn." More deer meant more than more deer. Slowly it became clear that it meant a disaster to the mountain.

Nature, Leopold came to realize, is not like a set of isolated boxes. It is like a line of dominoes falling, one after the other. To repeat the process described above, but in more detail: fewer wolves and panthers did mean more deer; more deer, however, meant exhaustion of the "browse" on which deer feed; exhaustion of browse meant that deer would turn toward "second choice" plants; the exhaustion of these meant deer would turn to the only remaining food, the forest trees, which would first be grazed for leaves and stems, and finally for their bark; the eating of bark would lead to "girdled" trees, which soon died; the dead trees, in turn, loosened their grip on soil already denuded of substory plants; water-absorbing soils, leaf-mulch, subsoils, and gravels eroded downhill, exposing bare rock, increasing flooding, and silting once pristine creeks and rivers; fish populations quickly declined. Who would have thought that shooting a wolf would kill a fish?

This particular chain of causes and effects was not, it turned out, limited to the Southwest. As time went on it became omnipresent, reaching throughout the United States wherever the extirpation of predators (and well-meant practices like the winter feeding of deer) resulted in the drastic increase of deer populations. The environment on which deer subsisted inevitably declined. And there was yet another negative effect. Lack of food and lack of predation soon produced dwarfed, deformed, or sick deer herds. Who would have thought that killing a predator would deform a deer? Yet it was true: predators, which subsisted on the old, the sick, and also the young, are necessary to the health of the deer herd.

What was true of predator extermination proved true of any number of other practices designed to "improve" the environment. Common wisdom, which Leopold originally accepted, had it that more rather than less cattle grazing was necessary on grasslands in and near national forests: more, even if that meant going to extremes! This view rested on an assumption which seemed unshakable. Grass, it was argued, was a dangerous carrier of fire, introducing it first into the edges, then by contagion into the center, of the forest. It followed from this—a theorem which stockmen were glad to apply—that overgrazing was not a menace but a blessing in disguise.

This, too, turned out not to be true. Not only are native grasses less of a threat to fire-prone forests than had been believed: grass is an extremely important stabilizer and protector of watersheds. To take only one example—a tragedy which Leopold knew well—overgrazing of native grasses in New Mexico's Blue River watershed left the rich soils there unprotected. Serious flooding then reduced the once verdant valley to a place of bare rocks, gravel, and sand. Its economic value, its game, and its natural beauty were all lost in a handful of years.

Leopold's approach to grass and to the policy of methodical overgrazing was to be reversed almost immediately—by 1915, in fact, when he stated his changed opinion publicly and endeavored to put it into effect in the national forests. (You have more to gain, he argued, from protecting the grass and letting it do its job than you have to gain from overgrazing: or than you have to lose from propagation of fire.) His attitude toward predators, by contrast, changed only slowly. It is fascinating to follow this sea-change in attitude in the course of his writings. By the 1920s occasional doubts were beginning to appear in speeches and articles; by the 1930s—especially after a fateful trip to Germany in 1935—he began to reverse his previous stand; by the 1940s he was openly arguing for the reintroduction of predators, wherever possible, into their former habitats. By then he was the center of a furious debate in Wisconsin over deer policy and deer hunting regulations.

Reversal of opinion on these and many other specific issues (for example, on the still thorny issue of fire suppression) was accompanied in Leopold by a still broader shift. The Pinchot-Roosevelt "Highest Use" doctrine rested on the assumption that government, using what would more accurately be called industrial than "scientific" techniques, can through this technology protect and augment a wide range of natural resources. The pressure of events—the history of the use of these industrial or quasi-industrial methods—increasingly demonstrated their inadequacy. Something was wrong.

Leopold's opinion shift was accelerated in the mid-1930s, as was briefly noted above, by a study, in Germany, of the German system of forestry and game management. In 1924 he left his Forest Service position in New Mexico for a job as assistant (later associate) director of the U.S. Forest Products Laboratory at Madison, Wisconsin. The almost exclusively industrial horizons of the laboratory, however, increasingly frustrated Leopold, who resigned in 1928. The next five years were spent in a variety of activities, including game surveys of the Midwestern states, erosion control work for the Civilian Conservation Corps, and the writing and publishing of his *Game Management*, destined to be a classic in its field for decades. In 1933 he took a position as chairman of game management in the Department of Agricultural Economics at the University of Wisconsin. In 1939 he became chairman of a new Department of Wildlife Management there. The trip to Germany took place from June to December, 1935.

The results of German forestry and wildlife management policy shocked Leopold. Germany seemed to have bent all its efforts to producing only trees, and to populating its standing tree reserves with only deer. Compared to American forests the German tree preserves were barren, and the increasing deer populations beginning to become apparent in the "States" had for many years already posed a serious problem there. In the words of Susan L. Flader (1974):

> The consequences of artificially maintained deer populations were many. Almost intolerable browsing pressure prevented reproduction of the most palatable browse species. Leopold estimated that at least two-thirds of the plant species normally occurring in the German forests had been "run out" by deer. . . . In addition to yew, deer were eliminating raspberry, blackberry, other palatable berries, and the forest game birds, as well as wildflowers and songbirds.

Not only did the German approach lead to the suppression of biological diversity. As was beginning to appear in North America, extirpation of predators, hunting policies, and habitat deterioration led to a deterioration of the health of the deer here also. Poor antler development and significant weight loss, Leopold observed, were common.

Such facts—and they were incontestable—weighed heavily in Leopold's thought. His German experience, brief though it was, made several things clear. First, it was impossible to pursue wildlife policy apart from forest policy. The two were interlocked; any attempt to deal with one without the other could only lead to destruction. More generally, the situation in Germany's *Dauerwald* was foreboding. North America's forests were still rich, diverse, prolific. If the lessons of Teutonic forestry were not learned, however, a sad fate awaited America's woods. No longer wild, no longer rich, they would be reduced to little more than tree farms populated by domesticated game.

It would be an exaggeration to say that this experience marked the "turning point" in Leopold's thought. His view of the world had always been marked by change; the elements of his thought had always rested on a number of concrete experiences (overgrazing, watershed problems, deer overpopulation) having specific dates in his life. Perhaps it would be fair to say that what Leopold learned in Europe was a catalyst, drawing together threads in his thought in radically new ways. Humankind, he now began to believe, confronts experience in a misleading way, thinking as if people were the center of the world. The reverse, he now saw, is true. This insight is what he tried to capture in his dictum that rather than thinking short-term and human-centered, we should learn to "Think like a mountain." Many have had a rocky time trying to figure out just what "thinking like a mountain" means. In at least two respects, as we hope to show, what Leopold meant is very clear.

To "think like a mountain" is, first of all, to think in the long run: not just for a year, and, in many contexts, not just for a generation. Human life cycles are brief compared to the immense temporalities of ecosystems; but it is those temporalities with which we must deal. What, over the very long haul, will happen to the valley, the prairie, the mountain? To answer this question one must be able to think not only in the long run but in terms of a vast, intricate, interconnected web of living causes and effects. Predator affects deer affects tree affects soil affects watershed affects fish. Cattle affect grass affects soils affect streams affect fish. Fish affect birds affect insects affect plants. The mountain is not just a heap of rocks on which various species of living things happen to be scattered. It is a dynamic, interactive system—almost an organism—through which effects and counter-effects cycle and counter-cycle. To think like a mountain is to attempt as fully as possible to understand all of this living webwork and to try to structure one's actions in terms of it. It is never to think of one's actions in terms of only a few isolated factors (for example: predator elimination and deer population). It is to be both realistic and "holistic" at the same time.

But something else is involved. To think like a mountain is to go beyond one's simply human viewpoint, to view the world not in terms of human projects alone but in terms of the cycles and mutual supports that make up the world. This will at first seem strange: perhaps inhuman. But the goal is not to deprive anyone of their humanity; it is to see that humanity is one among a family of organisms, all of which depend upon each other and upon the stability of sun, water, wind, and earth. Probably even more difficult for us than the belief that we are part of a family of creatures is the stricture that we must learn to think long-term. Most of us think not much farther ahead than our children and grandchildren. To think like a mountain is to think ahead hundreds, even thousands, of years.

In his years at the University of Wisconsin Leopold, if he wished to learn how to think like a mountain, was to spend most of his time thinking like an executive and a committee chairman—a very different thing. Given the demands of his position and his many activities, it is hard to imagine how he found time to think at all. But in the midst of organizing his new department, helping to found the Wildlife Society and the Wilderness Society, and serving a six-year term on the Wisconsin Conservation Commission, he managed to constantly rethink his assumptions, probing the limits, reshaping his view of people and nature.

He also managed to do something which, retrospectively, was to change the way we view him and to form the occasion of some of his best writing. Students of Wisconsin geography point out that this state has several distinct regions. Among these are the Sand Counties: cutover, worn-out lands, much of which by the time Leopold arrived in Wisconsin had reverted to the state for lack of payment of taxes. The Sand Counties in those years reminded many observers of the 1930s Dust Bowl of Texas, Oklahoma, and Kansas: a sprawling landscape of leached soils and depleted, often deserted, farms. Here in 1935 Leopold acquired a river-bottom farm to which he could retire for reflection, and which he and his family were gradually to rebuild, bringing back native grasses and wildlife and forests. It is this farm and its environs that Leopold was to celebrate in *A Sand County Almanac*: the farm, the environs, and the sometimes hard lessons they taught.

Curt Meine (1988), Leopold's biographer, draws a graphic picture of the farm as Leopold first saw it:

> . . . there were few pines in sight. Clumps of aspens sprouted along the margin of a frozen marsh. A haggard row of wind-swept elms lined a driveway. The fields, poor and sandy even in the summer, seemed even more barren when gripped by winter. The spent soils supported only sand burrs, their dried heads held out above the snow. The farmhouse at the end of the line of elms had burned down; all that remained of the house was a dug-out foundation. To one side there was a small but sturdy chicken coop, the only structure still standing on the property.

Starting with nothing but the frame and walls of the chicken coop, the Leopolds and their four children were to build a sturdy house ("the shack," as they called it) capable of sheltering them and occasional visitors. They planted thousands of pine seedlings and dozens of shrubs on the once barren property—mountain ash, juneberry, nannyberry, cranberry, raspberry, plum—replanting again when dry years killed off their plantings of a previous spring. They took up the experiment of "banding" birds to keep a check on their travels and life cycles, and began studying bird behavior. The Wisconsin River, which flowed past their property, made a rich habitat for ducks and geese, which the Leopolds observed at length—and hunted.

Leopold's affection for the sandy-soiled farm matured along with his knowledge of it. His journals, originally scanty, increasingly teem with detailed notes on birds, weeds, trees, wildflowers, grapevines, deer, rabbits, hawks, wading birds, migratory waterfowl, foxes. Affection for Leopold did not mean sentimentality. How animals died, what they preyed on, the brevity of their lifetimes in the wild, and the disruptions caused by fires, droughts, and severe cold fill his handwritten pages, as do the quandaries of restoring and managing land. One species of tree, if widely planted, might favor some species of birds or small mammals; but it might rule out others. Or if some sorts of trees were to survive and grow, a campaign would have to be mounted to hunt the rabbits which stripped the saplings. Land management had more than its share of dilemmas. Knowledge was never complete.

Almost from the beginning the land had been mistreated: first by wheat, then by misguided drainage schemes. The enthusiastic growing of wheat—for which the Sand Counties were scarcely suited—ground to a halt there as in most of Wisconsin by the end of the 1870s. Exhausted soils, helped along by wheat rust and hordes of insects, spelled the end of one excess. A generation later it was followed by a second. In the years 1910–1920, in the effort to create new farmland (having worn out the old), the marshes and other wetlands of central Wisconsin were cut by deep ditches: vast rectangles steam-shoveled into peaty lowland soils. Though at the time it seemed like a marvelous idea, Leopold (1970) explains what happened:

> But crops were poor and beset by frosts, to which the expensive ditches added an aftermath of debt. Farmers moved out. Peat beds dried, shrank, caught fire. Sun-energy out of the Pleistocene shrouded the countryside in acrid smoke. No man raised his voice against the waste, only his nose against the smell. After a dry summer not even the winter snows could extinguish the smoldering marsh. Great pockmarks were burned into field and meadow, the scars reaching down to the sands of the old lake, peat-covered these hundred centuries. Rank weeds sprang out of the ashes, to be followed after a year or two with aspen scrub.

The result of this massive failure was probably predictable. Only reflooding of the newly drained areas could stop the peat fires. An epoch of reflooding thus began as ditches were plugged and filled and bogs and marshes slowly began to refill. Gradually the acrid smoke pall died away. A depleted nature struggled to reassert itself.

What the Leopolds managed to do with their worn-out farm is now termed restoration ecology: a "new" field from which much is expected in a world of mistreated land and diminished resources. But, as Leopold realized with increasing clarity, if people know how to restore the land or how not to mistreat it in the first place, that is no guarantee that they will do so. Nor will the mere passing of laws accomplish the task. Humankind was up against an entirely new situation in its relations to nature. Always in the past it had managed to overcome challenging—and threatening—new situations with changes of viewpoints and values. A similar change was needed now, Leopold saw. It was time for a new, broadly moral revolution, this time directed not toward other human beings alone, but, more broadly, toward the land.

A Land Ethic: Its Structure and Meaning

"Thinking like a mountain" is a useful and expressive phrase. It speaks both of hard, gritty reality and ultimate wisdom. Unfortunately, it is extremely general. It needs content; it needs something to help us deal with the specifics—the particular situations—of the world. Leopold moves in this direction by pointing toward three fundamental characteristics of nature that must be respected if our environment is to have a chance. These are: integrity, stability, and beauty. We will examine here what these terms mean, both in a general and a practical sense.

Integrity. Inherent in a land ethic is a sensitivity to place, both to the concrete particulars of the land as well as to ecosystemic processes. Integrity refers not to the economic value of the land as resource (a quantity that can be measured), but to a sometimes incommensurable quality of nature: that is, wholeness. The English word "integrity" comes from the Indo-European root *tag* and, in turn, the Latin derivative, *integer*, meaning whole, untouched. Even so, the scientific question of what constitutes integrity is hard to answer. Through research in the desert Southwest, and later in the farmlands of the American Midwest, Leopold came to appreciate wholeness not as a characteristic restricted to totally natural, that is, wild, landscapes, but as an ideal that could also be achieved in humanized landscapes.

A "whole" ecosystem is not necessarily undeveloped, but rather is one uncorrupted by development, one that even though used for human purpose remains unimpaired, sound. Such an ecosystem is able to sustain itself through adverse circumstances, not only natural cycles such as drought, but human disturbances as well. Guided only by economic criteria, humans characteristically make radical alterations—clearcutting a forest, overgrazing pasture land, damming free-running rivers—that cumulatively change, disrupt, fragment, and ultimately destroy vital links in the web of life. Ecological dysfunction confirms the limits of exclusively economic thinking: nature does not recognize humanly imposed boundaries and categorical schemes.

Of course, the importance of integrity is not news to ecology-minded Texans, such as wildlife professionals, who have long recognized that the consequences of traditional land use can be ecologically devastating. Joel Wooldridge (1982) argues that the frontier outlook is manifest in "the negative attitude toward land-use controls" that pervades "the Texas legislature, the governor's office, and state agencies. . . ." Elected politicians and appointed officials claim, Wooldridge continues, that environmental values and economic goals are balanced. "In actuality, evidence is available all over Texas to demonstrate poor urban land-use decisions made to gratify the desire for short-term economic gains at the expense of environmental quality." Which is to say, Texans today have few examples of large-scale ecosystems possessing integrity in the strongest sense of that term.

Centuries of human practice cannot be changed overnight. Neither can Texas history or the frontier mentality. The Big Thicket of Southeast Texas, once a vast, cohesive wild community, is now crisscrossed by oil pipelines and power right-of-ways, drowned under new lake water, deeply scarred by clearcuts. It has very nearly lost its biological integrity (see Gunter 1971). Similarly, the carving-up and elimination of extensive "cedar" forest in the Texas Hill Country threaten the existence of one of Texas' rarest birds, the golden-cheeked warbler (*Dendroica chrysoparia*), while piecemeal clearcutting the national forests of East Texas drives the red-cockaded woodpecker (*Picoides scalaris*) toward extinction. Habitat is no longer habitat when only fragments of it remain. Whatever the measure of "wholeness," every conservationist knows that it is a vanishing species, not only in the Big Thicket, but almost everywhere else in Texas. The high plains of West Texas. The bottomlands of the Brazos. The wetlands of the Texas coast. The once continuous forests of the "Post Oak Belt." The Piney Woods of East Texas.

The fragmentation of forests provides a clear case of the loss of integrity, as these examples suggest. So also does the fragmentation of wetlands or the interruption of rivers or smaller streams. A forest of a thousand acres will support a large number of plant and animal species: birds, insects, mammals, reptiles, overstory and understory trees. If it is broken up into three or four pieces (of, say, 150 acres each) separated from each other by pasture or subdivisions, nature's wealth immediately declines. The number of animal species declines, along with the number of individuals. The wood thrush may continue to exist, but one will see fewer of them. Birds like the bluebird and the oriole may disappear, to be replaced by the cowbirds that now are able to practice "nest piracy": to lay their eggs in formerly unreachable bluebird and oriole nests, nests which will be taken over by the cowbird young (which unceremoniously push the oriole and bluebird nestlings overboard). As with bluebirds, so with deer and fox and moths and wildflowers. All creatures, great and small, require a habitat of sufficient size and structure. Fragment the size, fragment the structure, and they are gone.

Stability. Integrity and stability are not unrelated: integrity concerns the wholeness of ecosystems, while stability concerns the ability of ecosystems to maintain themselves. If the integrity of an ecosystem is impaired, so, too, is its stability. Of course, even natural (unhumanized or relatively undeveloped) ecosystems are dynamic. Stability does not mean invariance. It means the capacity to survive extremes of climate or soil change or disease. It is defined by nature's ability to respond to stress effectively.

Stability is difficult to measure, and insofar as the term has been associated with the balance of nature, it is a controversial concept. Some ecologists argue that environmentalists have misinterpreted nature, neglecting its inherent dynamism in the effort to impose ideological, unecological preservationist schemes. Clearly, contemporary environmental scientists cannot provide entirely adequate measures of stability, nor can they predict (in the strong sense, down to the last grain of dust or the last plant growth association) the effect of human actions upon either natural or humanized ecosystems. Yet scientists know enough to say that the human species collectively runs the risk of breaking itself on the wheel of its own misdeeds. The uncertainty of scientific measurement and the conjectural nature of prediction do not do away with ecological reality. Environmental science knows with certainty that human beings are upsetting the stability of nature's economy.

In areas of Texas where French tamarisk (saltcedar, *Tamarix gallica*), juniper forest ("cedar brakes," *Juniperus* spp.), mesquite (*Prosopis glandulos*), and other water-absorbing brush have overtaken former grasslands, once permanent streams now flow only in wet periods and are dry in rain-free months. The ecosystems which would have been sustained indefinitely in those streams—for bodies of water have ecosystems, too—inevitably perish. (As in the case of the Concho River, removal of water-absorbing brush has allowed the water to run year-round again.) Similarly, for marginal farmlands in the western parts of the state: hard scrabble cotton farming, by dispersing and degrading thin layers of topsoil, led not only to the Dust Bowl of the 1930s, but to conditions in which today's grassland ecologies have never recovered their original richness and stability. *Though no biotic community can last forever, it is surely folly to destabilize and degrade ecologies which can serve us indefinitely, for centuries or millennia.*

Beauty. Texas, rivaled only by California and Alaska, is unsurpassed in the diversity of its natural beauty. Yet, beauty as a criterion for land use perhaps appears less plausible than either integrity or stability. To many people, beauty might seem subjective, anything but scientific. To anyone who places total faith in the market, the idea that considerations of beauty might override market-based decisions seems frightening. Beauty is simply not traded through the market—it has no use value (though states dependent upon tourists lured by scenic wonders tend to protect it).

Leopold, again, was a visionary in recognizing the importance, indeed, the centrality, of beauty to the land ethic. In part, beauty was a counterbalance to the unrestrained pursuit of profit. Leopold was not a foe of capitalism; but he was opposed to land use guided only by the profit motive. Environmental historians typically seize upon the apparent opposition between beauty and utility, believing that nature can either be exploited for its instrumental value or protected for its intrinsic value, but not both.

However, beauty and utility are not contradictories. For Leopold, the apparent opposition between beauty and utility, or between aesthetic preservationists and utilitarian conservationists, is just that: a matter of appearance rather than reality. To those informed by the land ethic—that is, an abiding comprehension of the land community and the relation of humankind to it—the choice between utility and beauty appears as a false dichotomy. Individuals will look at the land, Leopold writes, "as something more than a breadbasket." They "will see the beauty, as well as the utility, of the whole, and know the two cannot be separated" (quoted in Meine 1992).

As a rule, a beautiful landscape indicates a healthy ecosystem. Most of us would agree that a polluted stream with its dead fish and dumped garbage is ugly: certainly in comparison with a clean stream with clear waters, untrashed borders, and abundant life. Few would argue that a prairie reduced to sparse grass, weeds, and eroded earth is as beautiful as one richly covered with grass and wildflowers. To aim for natural beauty is thus often to produce a situation which is both ecologically and economically sustainable. To opt for ugliness is to choose a situation economically valuable to no one, or few.

Environmental aesthetics is just beginning to come of age. The impetus to consider aesthetics in land use is perhaps rooted in the human perception of natural beauty: art, so to speak, imitates nature. It is increasingly suspect to impose on natural ecosystems narrowly human criteria of beauty oblivious to the ecological dynamics of the land community. Today we find university departments of landscape architecture and even state highway departments attempting "to design with nature." Beauty may very well become a standard part of environmental impact assessments, so that land uses that impair natural beauty might be ameliorated, lessened, curtailed, or proscribed. Some nations, such as Finland, and states, such as Hawaii, are far ahead of Texas in thinking aesthetically. It is hard to see that they have anything to lose from it, and easy to imagine that they have a great deal to gain. If any people decides to save beautiful vistas, lovely stream courses, or fields of bluebonnets as a matter of principle, they will probably do well at saving their entire environment as a matter of fact. As Charles Eames has put it, "Who is to say that beauty is not useful?"

A skeptic would—and should—object that to prescribe beauty as an essential characteristic of an ideal environment may be to opt for merely cosmetic schemes which keep things looking good while the essential ecology dies. Lumber company "beauty strips" may improve the view on a drive from Athens to Livingston, but they hide the raw scars of clearcuts. The landscaping of a river or a lake may hide the fact that the waters are polluted, even devoid of life. Polluted air may sometimes make for beautiful blood-red sunsets, but that does not make up for the fact that the air is dangerous to breathe. We want to do more than Keep Texas Beautiful. We want to keep it resilient, and productive and healthy: clear down to the grass roots.

This objection is valid in a practical sense. Beauty—appearances—can be an excuse for covering up destructive ugliness. Leopold's ethics, however, cannot provide a basis for merely cosmetic solutions. For he provides us with not one but three criteria of environmental value. And he defines these (integrity, stability, and beauty) in terms of each other. Any natural beauty which merely dresses up appearances would on his terms be only skin deep. A beautiful forest would be a real, functioning forest capable of sustaining itself against extremes of climate or disease, not a thin strip of trees barely deserving the name "forest." A beautiful river would be one whose water not only glistens in the evening sun, but one which sustains life in its diversity and abundance. There are problems in relating integrity, stability, and beauty. But in remembering and applying them jointly we avoid one-sidedness and simplistic solutions.

What This Book Is Not

A great deal more could be said about these arguments. But our goal here is not so much to provide a scholarly treatise as to suggest some fundamental ideas for dealing with nature in positive and fruitful ways. If we continue the discussion here it is not to elaborate on stability, integrity, and beauty, but to make clear what *kind* of land ethics we are pursuing. There is more than one sort of land ethics. There are four, and this book tackles only one of them. The four are: land-reform ethics, land-rights ethics, land-use ethics, and land-community ethics. It is the last of these we propose here. But in order to understand land-community ethics it is necessary to explain the other three.

Land-reform Ethics. Land-reform ethics primarily involve considerations of justice and land. It is well known that a small percentage of Texans own a disproportionate percentage of the land. Marxists believe that this is inherently unethical, since wealth is used as an instrument of power to exploit lower classes of people. However, our framework is decidedly not Marxian. Our concern is primarily with the land abuses which occur because of disproportionate distribution of power. For example, wealthy Texans have ready access to the good land and wide open spaces that contribute to the quality of life. They avoid living in the vicinity of petrochemical plants or municipal waste disposal sites. In fact, it is no accident that toxic waste storage sites and dumps, or factories that emit toxics into the air and water, are usually located on the "wrong side" of town. Not only is land the cheapest on the wrong side of town, but the residents there are relatively disenfranchised in income, education, and political power. A recent study by the Texas Center for Policy Studies (Almanza et al. 1993) shows clearly and unequivocally that present land use raises serious questions of environmental equity.

Land-rights Ethics. Land-rights ethics primarily involve considerations of the intrinsic value of natural entities and ecosystems. Intrinsic value is the idea that, apart from whatever instrumental value nature has for human beings, it also has a value for itself. Support for the notion of intrinsic value comes from an assortment of sources, ranging from religious to scientific and philosophic. Responding to Lynn White's (1967) criticism that Jews and Christians caused the environmental crisis, primarily through the belief that God gave Man the right to dominate the earth, many Jewish and Christian leaders now argue that God gave humans the right only to care for the earth as good stewards: his blessing extends to all the creation. Scientific justification for intrinsic value has come from a variety of sources, such as systems theory and nonlinear thermodynamics. Ilya Prigogine (Prigogine and Stengers 1984), a University of Texas faculty member and Nobel Laureate, provides compelling arguments that natural systems are self-organizing, fully capable of goal-seeking behavior, rather than simply robots blindly following the mechanical laws of nature.

Land-use Ethics. Land-use ethics involve considerations that might be categorized as a reconsideration of the highest-and-best-use principle. Traditionally, land affairs in our state have been governed primarily by marketplace economics and secondarily by state and local government. By long tradition, the owners of land have been accorded numerous legal privileges, among which are the rights to possess, to use, and to manage. Government at various levels has regulated these rights through a variety of means, including permitting, zoning, taxation, and land-use planning. But, as a variety of studies show, a bottom-line, unecological mentality has largely dominated. (See Chapter 2 for specific examples.) Neither the market nor government has considered the actual costs, that is, the costs that have been absorbed by the land, of doing business. Land-use ethics thus reconsider, in a variety of ways, the decisions pertaining to the highest and best use.

Land-community Ethics. Our primary concern in this book involves land-community ethics. As a *point of departure*, we will begin—as is evident from what has already been written—with the best-known definition of a land ethic, the one proposed by Aldo Leopold. An action or behavior is right, he tells us, *when it preserves the integrity, stability, and beauty of the land community.* Our primary concern with land-community ethics does not mean that, as the case warrants, we do not also consider land-reform, land-use, or land-rights ethics. In truth, although each of these four kinds of land ethics can be distinguished in theory, in practice each begins to overlap with the others. We are not primarily interested in theoretical rigor per se (the kinds of arguments that ethicists make for other ethicists), but rather in offering to our fellow citizens—those who can see beyond narrowly economic interests—a framework that might help them begin to consider land issues more systematically and comprehensively. Consequently, when the definition of land ethics that we largely function within, that is, land-community ethics, runs into boundary questions with other kinds of land ethics, such as land-reform ethics, land-use ethics, and land-rights ethics, we will freely cross the boundary.

Windsurfer Tom Arnold
at Texas City Dike.

2

TEXAS: THE LAND AND ITS COMMUNITIES OF LIFE

If two words could be chosen to sum up the character of the Lone Star State, we would urge that they be "diversity" and "frontier." Few states are as diverse in soils, climate, and topography as Texas, and few remained frontier as long. Together these terms provide a striking image, suggesting hope. But they suggest problems, too: problems, and a future far different from the past, with its seemingly unlimited expectations. Of these terms we will deal first with diversity, the less known and less recognized of the two. Only later will we deal with limits—a third, increasingly evident, feature of the land.

Diversity

The tendency to picture Texas as the set of an immense Western movie—probably filmed in the deserts of California or Nevada—is slowly changing. Texas is a place not of endless similarity but of striking contrasts. Few have grasped the differences among the state's regions as effectively as the novelist Billy Lee Brammer (1986), who protested that a place so "muddled and various is hard to conceive as one entity":

> It begins . . . in an ancient backwash of old dead seas and lambent estuaries, around which rise cypress and pine thickets hung with spiked vines and the cheerless festoons of Spanish moss. Farther on, the earth firms: stagnant pools

are stirred by the rumble of living river, and the mild ferment of bottomland dissolves as the country begins to reveal itself in the vast hallucination of salt dome and cotton row, tree farm and rice field and irrigated pasture and the flawed dream of the cities. And away and beyond, even farther, the land continues to rise, as on a counterbalance with the water tables, and then the first range of the West comes into view: a great serpentine escarpment, changing color with the hours, with the seasons, hummocky and soft-shaped at one end, rude and wind-blasted at the other, blue and green, green and grey and dune-colored, a staggered fault line extending hundreds of miles north and south. . . . The land rises steeply beyond the first escarpment and everything is changed: texture, configuration, blistered facade, all of it warped and ruptured and bruise-colored.

The geologist Darwin Spearing (1991) paints the same panorama, but proceeding not from east to west but from the west eastward. To envision Texas, he states, one must see it

sweeping from volcanic mesas and thrusted mountains in the west, to red canyons of the Panhandle, along tropical sand barriers of the Gulf Coast, and across central limestone plateaus onto hard granitic terrain in the center of the state. Rocks of all ages, from crystalline gneiss of ancient Precambrian time to the loose sand of modern beaches, as well as every major rock type from igneous to metamorphic to sedimentary.

Some differences may not be obvious to the untrained eye, while in other cases to find a contrast one may have to take an extended drive. Still, the contrasts exist, everywhere, and with them abundant diversity.

In part this diversity is due to the sheer size of the state (roughly 800 miles north-south, 775 miles east-west). Even more, it is due to location. El Paso, in the west, is closer to Los Angeles than it is to Texarkana. Texarkana is nearer—by a factor of nearly two—to the Mississippi River than it is to the state capital at Austin. Brownsville is equidistant between San Antonio and Tampico and is closer to Mexico City than it is to Dallas (and is located as far south, incidentally, as the Florida Keys); Dalhart, in the northwest Panhandle, is closer to Cheyenne, Wyoming, than it is to Dallas (and has Colorado's climate). The Lone Star State thus sprawls from tropical Mexico to the High Plains, from the pines and cypress-tupelo swamps of the Deep South to the mesas and deserts of the American West. It is, almost, a geographical accident.

Confronted with this monument to diversity, geologists, ecologists, and geographers have proposed several different ways of dividing up the Lone Star State: according to landforms (topography), soil types, natural vegetation areas (roughly, bioregions), economic resources, and rainfall. For the purposes of this book we are going to take the state's eleven bioregions (well, eleven according to some authorities) and reduce them to seven. To these seven will be added an eighth: the Urban Sprawls, or Giant Slurbs, new human-made natural features which threaten to overwhelm the rest. We will start on the east with the Woodlands Region.

As large as Indiana and Maryland combined, the Woodlands Region consists of a western Post Oak Belt and an eastern Piney Woods. By and large, urbanization has bypassed this region, which remains a land of small towns and villages, removed from the hectic growth and social change of urban Texas and suspicious of it. This is a part of Texas that clearly fails to fit the image of the state. With a rainfall of over 30 to nearly 60 inches per year, with a history and an ethos linking it more to the Deep South than to the West or Midwest, the Woodlands resembles parts of Mississippi, Georgia, or the Carolinas.

Tending west from the Woodlands, the land becomes increasingly dry, increasingly "western." The Prairie Country, which sprawls from the eastern Panhandle all the way to the Post Oak Belt, contains roughly 12 million acres and receives between 20 and 35 inches of rain per year. The western reaches of the Prairie Country are devoted largely to cattle, the eastern reaches to cotton, other row crops, and cattle. Large areas of the region are beginning to be covered with urban sprawl. Authorities estimate that only 1 percent of it remains in its original state. Beyond the Prairie Country to the northwest lie the High Plains: a flat, unbroken land above the Caprock Escarpment, formerly home to vast ranching operations like the XIT and the T Anchor, now host to irrigation-based farms threatened by diminishing supplies of underground water.

South of the Prairie Country lie two regions markedly different from each other in topography, soils, and culture: the Brush Country and the Hill Country (the Edwards Plateau). Largely Hispanic in history and ethos, the Brush Country is a land of cattle, mesquite, catclaw, and sparse shade. The exception is the Lower Rio Grande Valley ("The Valley"), a winter refuge for snowbitten Midwesterners and a river-irrigated garden famous for its row and citrus crops. Due north of the sand and mesquite thickets of the Brush Country, the Hill Country rises abruptly. A limestone tableland deeply carved by creeks and rivers, the Hill Country is carpeted with a thick growth of cedar and liveoak. Though some valleys and other flatlands support farming, the Hill Country primarily sustains a stock industry of cattle, sheep, and—in its rockiest areas—goats. Many of its earliest settlers were German.

Another state region is the Trans-Pecos. It is dramatically different from any other part of Texas. Bounded by the Pecos River to the east, the looping, canyon-walled Rio Grande to the south, and New Mexico to the north, the land beyond the Pecos is a desert broken by spurs of the Rocky Mountains, getting as little as 8 inches of rain per year. Though dominated by the city-state of El Paso, with 600,000 denizens, it remains today thinly settled. Loving County, for example, boasts less than 200 residents. Though it contains both Big Bend and Guadalupe Mountains national parks and innumerable mesas, buttes, mountains, and canyons, the Trans-Pecos has its environmental problems. It appears that today no place is too remote or too thinly settled not to have them.

Finally, there is the Coastal Zone. Like the Woodlands, this region scarcely seems to belong to Texas. In spite of the state's 367-mile coastline, and in spite of the well-known cities in the area (Beaumont, Houston, Galveston, Victoria, Corpus Christi), the images of saltwater and of Texas seem impossible to blend. Palm trees, subtropical lagunas, and sandy beaches scarcely seem a backdrop for cowboys and cattle drives—though in fact the region, except for lushly vegetated stream courses meandering across its vastness, is largely prairie and has always supported cattle raising. The good news about the Coastal Zone includes the Aransas National Wildlife Refuge (winter home of the endangered whooping crane) and the Padre Island National Seashore. The bad news includes pollution from both petrochemical industries and cities, as well as the dual menace of development and urban sprawl. Many will be surprised that the Trans-Pecos has environmental problems; none—except the ignorant—will be surprised to learn that a land of refineries, ports, and large urban areas has its problems.

This brief sketch completes the review of the natural regions of Texas—except for a new, massive natural feature which needs to be added to any survey of the state. We refer to the Giant Slurbs. One of these stretches from north of Dallas–Fort Worth down the Blackland Prairie to Waco and Austin through San Antonio; the other reaches from Corpus Christi to Houston to Beaumont and Galveston, and then from Galveston through Houston to Conroe. These areas are not one single "slurb" development. But they are on the march. As the maps show, they extend their tentacles along the interstates and bind together urban areas once thought of as unlinked and unrelated. When the authors of this book were boys, such an entity did not exist. Now, already, it is two-thirds made. By the time the authors depart this mortal realm—well in the future, we hope—it will be 100 percent complete, and continuous, *and still growing.*

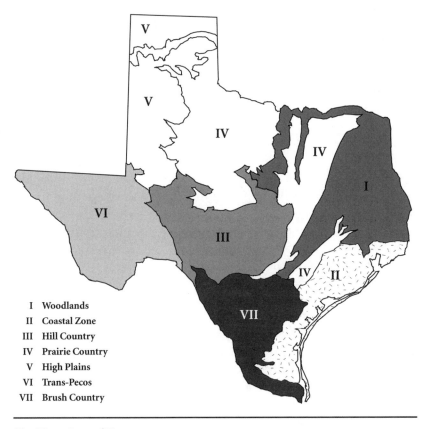

I   Woodlands
II   Coastal Zone
III   Hill Country
IV   Prairie Country
V   High Plains
VI   Trans-Pecos
VII   Brush Country

The Bioregions of Texas

It might be argued that this is not a very surprising development, or, in the long run, very important. What has come late to the Lone Star State, it will be said, has already happened in the industrial Northeast, the Great Lakes region, and California. Vast, disorganized urban sprawl is part of the modern world, and we should simply get used to it.

We will not argue the point here. One of the significant things this study can do, besides arguing the issues pro and con, is to point out, simply, *that there are issues.* The Urban Sprawls or Giant Slurbs are coming into existence with few Texans knowing about them, much less pondering the results. A book about how land is, will be, or ought to be used could not be complete if it did not paint a picture of massive, regionwide urban spread.

Predictably, this diversity also translates into politics. The goals of water-starved West Texas and of water-rich East Texas not only differ, they lead to outright conflict, as East Texans struggle to hold onto water resources West Texans covet. The economy of the Piney Woods, dependent on timber harvest, scarcely coincides with the desire of urban multitudes in the Great Slurbs for wilderness experience and open space. The outlook of ranchers on the High Plains diverges significantly from those of executives managing the petrochemical industries of the Coastal Zone. The problems of an environmentally and economically many-faceted state seem to fly apart from each other, as by centrifugal force.

Frontier

There is another, deeper problem, however: the reality, and the mystique, of the frontier. One of the authors of this book is descended from Kansas settlers, the other from Texas surveyors and ranchers. It is easy for them to understand the Lone Star State's pride in its frontier experience, and many of the values—of independence, and practical good sense—that stem from it. The trouble is, however, that the idea of the frontier hangs on—*but the frontier is over.* It is vitally necessary to rethink our real and pressing present situation and not to confuse it with a situation that is past.

"Texas" and "frontier" so easily associate that to some they seem almost one word. From the first Spanish settlements (1760) through the first Anglo pioneers (1820) until well into the twentieth century (until roughly the end of the First World War in 1918), the Lone Star State remained frontier in the most traditional sense: a land frontier, with still untouched acreage to commandeer and develop. When its first Anglo settlers broke land in the Brazos Valley in 1820, large areas of Mississippi were being settled; when ranches were being created in the Trans-Pecos in the 1890s, the last free lands of Montana and the Dakotas were being fenced. For over a hundred years the state possessed ungrazed prairie to browse, unbroken land to plow, and virgin forests to cut. People still live who can remember the ending of this, the traditional frontier, which was not only long in number of years, but relatively recent. (Compare it, for example, with Iowa, traversed by the frontier and completely settled in twenty years.) It is all too easy for Texans to imagine—as could successive generations of their ancestors—that there is more land out there, somewhere, waiting to be settled.

Important as the land frontier is to the mind of Texas, it provides only one component of the frontier mentality. The other is provided by a series of resource booms—four of them, or even five—starting with cotton, then cattle, then timber and oil, then cotton again, booms which overlapped and which, though now ended, still leave the impression that there is "more where that came from," that another resource boom (in oil or natural gas, for example) is just around the corner. When King Cotton was temporarily deposed at the end of the Civil War, Texans were able to round up thousands of longhorn cattle running wild in the Brush Country and head them north to the railheads of Kansas. The result was a cattle boom that rolled into the 1880s and gave the state resource capital that the other states of the Confederacy desperately lacked. When the cattle boom subsided, the slow recovery of cotton farming in the state was joined by a timber harvesting boom in the state's Woodlands. Texas—a little-known fact—worked its way up to become one of America's largest timber producers. When timber production peaked, around 1910, an oil boom was emerging and flourishing, beginning at Spindletop in 1900 and spreading northward and westward into the 1940s: a boom in oil production which, in turn, spawned new industries for the refining and transportation of oil and oil products. Accompanying this last hurrah, and reaching its peak in the 1950s, the growth of irrigated farming and the westward movement of cotton production brought a new prosperity to the High Plains.

Oil in particular ties the series of economic booms to the last years of the land frontier. Oil boom towns had the chaotic, exuberant jostle of Kansas railhead towns during the heyday of the cattle drives or of San Francisco during the Gold Rush. As adventurers flocked from all over the world to Batson or Ranger or Corsicana or Burkburnett, fortunes were made or lost on the toss of a coin or the fluke of a gusher or a dry hole. We recall the story of a man whose gold watch was stolen during the Burkburnett oil boom; furious, he went around the block, stole a gold watch from a man he had never seen before—and got his watch back! Such tales and times brought the romance of the land frontier and its expectations of infinite horizons well into the twentieth century and well within living memory.

The attitudes of frontiering people are well documented. One thinks, in this regard, of Walter Prescott Webb's *The Great Frontier* (1953), but there have been many similar studies, both formal and informal, such as Larry McMurtry's *In a Narrow Grave* (1968). Among the basic characteristics of the frontier mind are: an easy expectation of surplus, a casual contempt for caution, an exaggerated, at times fanatical individualism, and a crusty, sometimes unhinged anti-intellectualism.

The frontier, Webb once remarked, was fanatically narrow. He could have added that it was narrowest where books and ideas are concerned. The Puritans landed at Plymouth Rock in 1620; by 1636 they had already founded Harvard University. By contrast, English-speaking Texas began to be settled along the lower Brazos River Valley in 1820; but by 1900 the state had only one public library: on Galveston Island. (The location, by the way, is telling; Galveston was never quite considered part of the state by

Texans, who thought of it as a safe offshore refuge for gambling, pirates, houses of ill repute, and ideas.) It is true that by 1858 an embryonic University of Texas was founded. But the purposes of higher education in Texas can best be found in the names of its universities: Texas Agricultural and Mechanical College, Grubbs Vocational College (now the University of Texas at Arlington), Texas Technological College, Lamar Technical College, Texas Agricultural and Industrial College. There is nothing wrong with technology per se: our present society could scarcely survive without it. But such schools were hardly centers of common learning where the shapes of possible futures could be debated. Dedicated to immediate practical results, they were—and were long to remain—opaque to possibilities, negative toward ideas.

When a strong tendency to be closed to ideas is joined to the strong expectation that, whatever one is exploiting, there will be "plenty more where that came from," the results can be unfortunate. Why limit the hunting of bears in the Piney Woods when there have always been bears and presumably always will? Why limit the withdrawal of underground water on the High Plains when one appears to be sitting atop an ocean of water? Why develop oil resources cautiously when there is a boom going on, keeping Texas prosperous while the rest of the nation suffers through a Great Depression? Why listen to a bunch of Ph.D. biologists when one has been raised to believe that such people, besides being pretentious, are completely lacking in common sense? And why put up with laws and regulations which, insidiously, destroy one's freedoms: freedoms which, ideally, should be absolute and without exception?

Such questions are understandable, and not without point. College professors are not always right. Not all laws are well written, and, even if well written, well enforced; and not all hindrances to behavior are more help than hindrance. But in every region of the state it is a simple matter to point to the costs of the heedless exploitation of nature, undertaken at breakneck speed and with contempt for any crazy person who might argue against it. These negative, often needless effects will be explored in detail in the next chapter. But it will be helpful to point out a few of them here.

A drive through the Woodlands of eastern Texas may provide green vistas, the sight of blue lakes, and the smell of pines. But most of us do not know how to look farther. The tall trees and dense growth at the edge of the highway are liable to be "beauty strips": thin lines of forest left along the highways, as we have already noted, to mask massive clearcutting. The results of clearcutting—to be discussed in Chapter 6, on the Big Thicket— are sterile forests, agricultural operations which grow lines of pine trees exactly like rows of corn. In such artificial ecosystems, ferns, flowering trees, orchids, wildflowers of all kinds, birds, and most forms of game find it impossible to flourish. But as noted above, little of this is visible from the road. Nor is the downgrading of local streams, which accumulate silt as runoff from clearcutting operations.

A drive along the Coastal Zone provides equally hopeful views. Here endless prairie, under drifting clouds; there sandy rivers, creeks, and bayous meandering through natural forest corridors; there salt marshes and bays glittering in the afternoon sun, beaches sprawling tawny and white under swarms of pivoting gulls. Except for the growing, still occasional spread of urban development, from the road things seem to be much as they always were.

But from the road a lot of things are not clear. It is not clear that the damming of rivers far upstream deprives the bays and estuaries of the fresh water they need for their health, or that the same dams deprive the barrier islands—those long, thin islands stretching along the coast, that protect the mainland from tropical storms—of the "sand budget" they need to sustain themselves. It is not clear that urban sprawl and industrial growth along the coast have proceeded unplanned, without forethought, so that pollution becomes a danger not only for fisheries but for vacationers in the region. It is not clear that in the Houston-Galveston area some 200,000 people have been allowed to live at sites 20 feet above sea level or less: though the tides from a full-blown tropical hurricane are liable to reach 20 feet or more. It is not even clear—what a brief walk along the beach usually makes evident—that the beaches themselves are increasingly strewn with garbage brought in from the Gulf, including especially lumps of "tar": congealed crude oil dumped from the bowels of boats and barges.

So, too, for the High Plains. A drive from Canyon to Muleshoe or Lubbock to Dalhart will suggest a world much as it has been for decades: small towns surrounded by endless plains, ranchland interspersed with farmland, the ranch and farm houses remote from each other and sheltered by tall, spreading hardwood trees that one suspects have been nursed through many a long, dry summer. On the farmland irrigation machinery stands idly or revolves, tossing bright, sparkling water into the air. The smell of irrigation water, sometimes tinged with the scent of insecticide or liquid fertilizer, drifts through the car windows. Turn on that car radio. Pick up that country and western station. Feel good.

Only, far underground, a problem grows, casting its shadow over a sunny land. The water which has funded the lucrative agriculture of the High Plains flows from the Ogallala Aquifer, a stratum of fresh water laid down long ago and stretching from Texas clear to Nebraska. The Ogallala once seemed inexhaustible, but in recent years the reality of limits has begun to dawn, putting a severe dent in the concept of limitless expansion. Irrigation has worked here by mining underground water as if it were a seam of coal. Like coal, once the resource is gone it will not return. Hence the lowering of water tables throughout the region—all the way to Nebraska. Hence the decline of irrigated agriculture in some areas and its disappearance in others. Hence the very real possibility of depopulation in the High Plains. With careful husbanding of water resources from the beginning—that is, with a different philosophy—this might have been prevented; unquestionably it could have been forestalled for many decades. As it is, West Texans have begun to become accustomed to the bumper sticker proclaiming WILL THE LAST PERSON LEAVING AMARILLO PLEASE TURN OUT THE LIGHTS?

The same is true for each of the regions of the Lone Star State. From the highway, from the mall, from the new suburbs, very little appears to be wrong. In reality: in the soils, the streams, the air, the underground strata, many things go wrong, and become increasingly so. The old reality remains only in appearance. The old abundance runs aground, on a rock of undeniable scarcity. Once a virgin land, Texas has become a land of neglect. This is a new reality. It will not go away. Not just philosophy but sheer common sense calls on us not to fall into denial of the hard facts. It is necessary to explore, and to face them.

*Manuela Dominguez, Mary Alcorn,
Irma and Chuy Dominguez atop El Diablo Plateau,
Hudspeth County, overlooking proposed Texas
Low Level Radioactive Waste Disposal Site.*

3

TEXAS: A STATE OF NEGLECT

Some Texans pride themselves on having "anti-environmental" attitudes. We recall the 1970s era bumper stickers that flourished during the energy crisis: DRIVE 70; FREEZE A YANKEE. Energy conservation was *not* for Texans. Ranchers often protest the protection of endangered species, which, from their point of view, violates the sanctity of private property. Farmers become angry because their water rights are brought under the scrutiny of state agencies. Industrialists object to the imposition of air quality, noise abatement, and similar environmental provisions, arguing that these are too costly. Workers, believing that stringent environmental regulations will cause productive enterprises to close or move elsewhere, fear for their jobs.

As educators we know firsthand that changing attitudes is always a slow process. Certain attitudes dominate simply because of history and economics: modern Texas was built on the exploitation of natural resources, boom following upon boom with the busts soon fading from memory. Things have changed somewhat, but far more so than attitudes. Manufacturing, including the petrochemical industry, is the largest single sector of the economy (approximately 16 percent). The service sectors, followed by finance, insurance, and real estate, are nearly as large (approximately 14 percent each). Mining is fifth (approximately 10 percent). And farming and ranching—amazingly—have fallen to eleventh place (generating less than 2 percent of the gross state product).

Walter Prescott Webb's *The Great Frontier* captures the attitudes of the original Texan, the hero who overcame all natural obstacles (Indians, wild lands, ferocious storms) and human limitations (fear, illness, human nature) in advancing civilization. Today, this archetype is still deeply impressed on many Texans. Trailing in the wake of the frontiersman, these youngsters become cowboys and cowgirls, roughnecks and truck drivers, even doctors and lawyers, aircraft workers and schoolteachers. And a few become entrepreneurs, movers and shakers that have propelled the Texas economy through boom after boom.

Yet the frontier is irrevocably behind us. The collapse of the oil patch and land market during the 1980s likely marks the end of economic booms based on the exploitation of natural capital. (Chapter 4 discusses how land ethics affect economic theory in the context of natural capital. The basic point is that when natural capital is abundant, such as old-growth forests awaiting the saw, virgin soil awaiting the plow, or oil fields awaiting discovery, the prices of timber, wheat, and petroleum are appropriately low. As natural stocks are depleted, however, the economic equation shifts. Price can no longer be used to determine the worth of natural capital.) But the dwindling of the natural resources that so many Texans have used for so long is only the visible face of the future. For Texans confront, as do all Americans, a land crisis that affects our atmosphere, our water, our flora and fauna: indeed, the stability of the global ecosystem itself.

Of course, the opinion of the public is shaped by the mass media. Citizens are lulled into complacency by televised events, perhaps showing the president visiting a Superfund cleanup site and expressing his concern. Such staged events make good photo ops, but do little to help us adjust our lifestyles to the complexities of the biosphere. Corporations spend billions of dollars generating images of themselves as "good environmental citizens," as exemplified by the nuclear power industry's campaign to position itself as offering the environmentally friendly energy technology. The fact that the mass media are mass, and owned by powerful multinational corporations with their own political agendas, is another source of concern. The mass media have the power both to create new and reinforce existing anti-environmental attitudes. On the one hand, we can do little about it. But we can attempt to overcome ecological illiteracy.

Nowhere is the lack of common understanding more clearly illustrated than in the gap between lay public perceptions of environmental crisis and scientific judgment. When typical citizens are polled on environmental risks, they respond (in rank order) as follows: Hazardous waste sites in use; hazardous waste sites not in use; stratospheric ozone depletion; worker exposure to toxic chemicals; radiation from nuclear power plants; industrial accidents releasing pollutants; radiation from radioactive wastes; pesticides harming farmers and agricultural workers; pesticide residues.

In contrast, ecologists and environmental scientists rank the highest risks as follows: Habitat alteration and destruction; species extinction and overall loss of biodiversity; global climate change (Loehr 1991).

Nothing, in our opinion, makes clearer the need for Texas land ethics, for a framework that provides evaluative criteria beyond those which are solely anthropocentric, that is, defined in terms of either economic efficiency or human health. If environmental issues are perceived by the public primarily as issues of human health and by industrial-political elites as primarily economic and engineering issues, then it is likely that humankind will never escape the myth of superabundance. The earth will continue to be conceptualized as a standing reserve for human economic appropriation. And environmental dysfunctions will continue to be conceptualized as simply technological challenges. Such conceptions, which are the dominant assumptions of what we call "mainstream environmentalism," are dangerously flawed.

Mainstream environmentalism shows little insight into the fact that human beings are part of the earth's natural biophysical processes—in two senses, both effecting and affected. Texas' major metropolitan newspapers now carry "air quality indices" in the weather section, alerting us when it's safe to breathe the air and when it's not. Less than two years ago Austin declared its first "ozone day." Residents of many areas are now paying inspection fees to ensure that their automobiles meet air quality standards. The open spaces and wild or semiwild lands that seemed to be within just a short walk for Texans growing up immediately before and after World War II are gone: woodlands cut, covered with apartments, and renamed "Quail Ridge"; wetlands drained and turned into federally subsidized wheat fields; creeks, rivers, and bottomlands diverted, channelized, or otherwise "improved" in the name of flood control.

The authors are well aware that only lengthy books, focused on a single theme, can adequately present the scientific details of land abuse. Our readers must bear in mind that we lack both the aspiration and the information required to provide baseline assessments in regard to even a single variable, whether water supply, air quality, or environmental toxics. The issues are so complicated that even specialists despair of mastering all the details. Nor do we pretend to offer adequate coverage of single bioregions and associated ecosystems. The goal of this chapter is simply to present *a credible overview* of the condition of the land (including both biotic and abiotic components) in the hope of raising ecological literacy in the context of Texas land ethics.

What we seem to need are stories about Texans in real places who articulate Texas environmental problems—real issues that unfold on the stage of history before our very eyes. One thinks in this regard of John Graves' book, *Goodbye to a River*, an intensely personal and detailed account of the cultural and ecological changes wrought by the damming of the Brazos River. Such a narrative helps urban dwellers in Austin and Dallas grasp the ecological implications of the water flowing from their taps. It comes from somewhere. And it has costs that go beyond the monthly water bill. But literally hundreds if not thousands of such books would be required to detail all of Texas. It would take a veritable army of authors, each of whom had lived for some time in a particular place in Texas, and understood it.

On the other hand, our account of Texas land ethics also appears to require enough distance from the particulars of place so that some sense of the larger issues, some grasp of general patterns facing Texas as a whole, emerges. It's pretty hard to care about global climate change when the seasons seem to come and go as always around Waxahachie or El Paso. Regardless, the fact is that global climate change isn't just an issue facing Africans living on the edge of the Sahara. Some computer models project that, given present trends, Texas in 2030 will be much hotter, a 3.4° F to 5.4° F increase in summertime temperatures on the average. Just as important is the projection that it will be a drier place, due to a northward shift of jet streams and increased evaporation. In Dallas the number of 100°+ summer days would increase from nineteen to seventy-eight; which would, of course, greatly increase consumers' electric bills and, ironically, the production of CO_2—a primary cause of climate warming—as a by-product of power generation. And this, serious as it is, barely scratches the surface. The effects of global warming on agricultural production and water use would be staggering.

In charting Texas as a state of neglect, therefore, we follow a perilous course between generality and specificity. Spatially considered, we range from issues that have global implications, such as climate change, to issues at the level of "neighborhood effects," such as toxics adversely affecting people who live near petrochemical plants. Much of our assessment offers an overview of the biophysical condition of the state of Texas; yet we often give particular emphasis to bioregional differences, consistent with the seven bioregions and the interlocking urban sprawl discussed in Chapter 2.

And we cover an expansive temporal range as well, dealing with near-term issues that are already upon us, as well as long-range issues that take Texas well into the next century.

Our readers are also warned that there is an *explicitly value-laden* component in our survey of the state of neglect. As noted in the Introduction, land ethics, as a recognizable area of concern, begin with Leopold's *Sand County Almanac.* But Leopoldian-inspired land ethics are revolutionary. The purview of this ethics extends far beyond the traditional bounds of exclusively human (that is, anthropocentric) concerns. Further, by arguing that the stability, integrity, and beauty of the land are good, and that these ecological criteria provide standards for evaluative judgment of human actions, Leopold crosses the line of purely "objective" ecology. In truth, as many ecologists, philosophers, and environmental scientists argue, the ironclad distinction once drawn between ecology and ethics, whatever utility that distinction might once have had, is rapidly losing its utility. Human judgment of ecosystem integrity and/or health is necessarily value laden.

Consider a single example. Was the damming of the Brazos River "progress"? Commercial development, including industry and real estate, followed in the wake of water resource projects, like those on the Brazos, and with this development came first thousands and then millions of immigrants. The population of post–World War II Texas was 7.2 million; by 1992 we had reached 17.6 million. Most of these new Texans are concentrated in the Giant Slurbs, the metropolitan areas that draw water from the reservoirs created over four or five decades of water resource development. (See Figures 1–6 below: by 2025 the Slurbs may become one megalopolis extending from San Antonio to the Red River.) The Texas boom, and the promise of the Sun Belt, could not be sustained without the technological intervention, the massive federal and state engineering projects, that changed the Texas landscape. One can argue that such changes are in fact within the normal order of nature, since nature itself is chaotic. It follows, on this line of argument, that human modification of the natural environment is not, in and of itself, an action any different than nature's own modifications.

Or, on the other hand, was the damming of the Brazos the end of a way of life, one more in tune with the land and the specific places that color the land, one on more intimate terms with the denizens of the land, the animals and the plants? Is it true that as civilization increases, the land necessarily suffers? Has the growth in the *quantity of life* made possible by resource development been accompanied by increases in the *quality of life*?

Clearly, water resource projects entail winners and losers. Large metropolitan areas and cities, like the Dallas–Fort Worth metroplex, are winners, with new water supplies assured for domestic, industrial, and municipal uses. Smaller communities and farming families are losers, displaced by land acquisition and economically marginalized by the new opportunities in metropolitan areas. And the bottomland itself (the geographic basin which holds the water), rough land that provides homes for countless plant and animal communities, is inundated by the conservation pool. Numerous studies suggest that economic development, while clearly enhancing the quantity of life, has done little to improve its quality. Texans, like Americans generally, seem to have more and enjoy it less. The virtually unrestrained population growth that manifests itself in urban sprawl has also been accompanied by a dramatic rise in disamenities, such as polluted air (more than half of all Texans breathe air that does not meet federal standards), noise, traffic jams (is it true that Dallas' North-central Expressway is the world's longest parking lot?), and crime.

From the vantage point of a land ethic, land-use issues go far beyond the usual purview of resource development and supply (the dynamic that, . for example, led to the damming of the Brazos) and human health (an equally potent dynamic that energizes the vast majority of our state's—and nation's—environmental policies). Clearly, a land ethic involves supply issues, such as the stock of potable water, clean air, and wild lands and creatures. But the focus of land ethics is not just on supply in relation to human beings, but supply in a broader, ecological sense. What, for example, did the damming of the Brazos do to the supply of water available for wild creatures and wild lands? How did the impoundment alter the entire watershed, including the diminishment of the flow of fresh water to the Gulf? Or of the sands which replenish the Gulf Coast's vital barrier islands? Even judged in their own terms as economically justified or necessary, do the impoundments on the Brazos adequately meet questions of supply? For whom? and for how long?

Second, land ethics also hinge (to a greater or lesser extent) on the notion that human action, whether public policy or the decision of individual consumers, is good if it preserves the integrity, stability, and beauty of the land community (see Chapter 1). The mainstream conservation movement in this country, progressive conservation or resource conservation, bases itself on the idea that conservation is nothing more than the wise (meaning primarily the efficient) use of natural resources. By introducing considerations of integrity, stability, and beauty we go beyond the purview of resource conservation. Resource conservation philosophy primarily evaluates in terms of cost-benefit analysis. But cost-benefit analysis assigns a discount rate to future values (that is, it assumes that they are irrelevant). On such terms nature can never escape the resource designation: it is a wasting entity.

For example, at a 7 percent discount rate, the future has no value beyond fifteen years. On this basis it is economically rational for the farmer making decisions about soil management, the logger making decisions about forest management, and the real estate developer building apartments to plan as if the end of the world will come in fifteen years. Why prevent soil erosion, when the farmer can invest his profits from this year's crops in areas bringing higher yields? A dollar of profit invested this year and compounded annually over fifteen years is worth a great deal more than a dollar earned in the tenth year. Or the fifteenth. And the same logic applies to clearcutting forests or developing raw land. The tragedy is that the economic rationality of discounting is ecologically irrational (Pimentel et al. 1995).

Finally, the land ethic is an ethic of humility. This in itself flies in the face of conventional wisdom. The cultural dynamic of Texas is technological and entrepreneurial. The movers and shakers of society, aided by engineers and technologists, believe that all problems can be resolved through human ingenuity and money. The land, so viewed, is little more than a testing ground for human ambition, a larder of raw materials to fuel the upward spiral of economic achievement.

The land ethic, in contrast, assumes a different posture. For one, although it recognizes that humans are actively engaged in productive processes that lead to economic transformations, it recognizes that certain fixities of existence, such as the Second Law of Thermodynamics, constitute real limits to even the best of our "movers and shakers." As a corollary, since time moves in one direction only, it follows that the land can be irreversibly damaged, that is, abused and even ruined in ways which foreclose the possibility of sustaining processes of economic transactions. This is an ethic not of cringing humility, but of an honest awareness of both human and natural limitations. On this basis the "movers and shakers" of society must set their actions in a frame of evaluation larger than mere short-term profit and expediency.

The State of Neglect

Our survey of the Texas land crisis is categorized under six headings: population, water, habitat modification, biodiversity, air, and waste. These appear to be independent. But they no more exist in splendid isolation from each other than do the various aspects of nature. Air quality is related to waste, since air pollution is a consequence of both the petrochemical industry and of the operation of automobiles—to only give two examples. Water supply is closely connected to population since—other factors being equal—more people require more water. Some environmental scientists believe that, since population has "ripple effects" strongly affecting the other five areas of concern, it is the most important issue facing Texans. Accordingly, we begin with population.

Population. Like Sergeant Friday in *Dragnet*, we want to begin with the facts, just the facts—in the world, then in Texas. In 1900 the world had one billion people. Present world population is approximately 5.6 billion, a total which, according to Dr. Paul Ehrlich of Stanford University, is twice the maximum *carrying capacity* of the planet for a sustainable human population. "Carrying capacity" is a technical term, roughly referring to the total number of human beings that could be biophysically sustained with adequate levels of nutrition, housing, and so on over hundreds if not thousands of generations.

Interestingly, those 5.6 billion people are 7.7 percent of all the humans that have ever lived. Roughly one-third of the present population lives in advanced industrial societies, enjoying historically unprecedented material abundance. Despite obvious problems of distribution, ample supplies of food, shelter, clothing, water—virtually all the amenities of life—are taken for granted, or nearly for granted, in these societies. The rest of the world, the so-called undeveloped and developing societies, perceiving the difference between their own quantity of life and that enjoyed in the developed world, aspire to Western standards of living. China, for example, is a developing nation, and has both the world's largest population (1.2 billion) and the highest rate of economic growth.

In one sense, world population issues are outside the purview of Texas land ethics. There seems to be little that Texans can do, even if they tried, to deal with population issues in Africa, Asia, or anywhere else. Not even the Texas Legislature can pass laws that will affect population policy in Rwanda or China. Yet the population of Rwanda, China, and all the other burgeoning nations across the world, affects Texans in many ways—ways which, though not immediately obvious, are very real.

Consider that in the rush to industrialize and provide Western-style amenities and standards of living for its citizens, China is mass producing refrigerators that utilize the CFC (chlorofluorocarbon) refrigerants: major contributors to the depletion of stratospheric ozone. Texans seem lucky so far, escaping the seasonal rotations of the ozone hole that expose humans as well as plants and animals to intense doses of infrared radiation. But this is a false security: if the rift in stratospheric ozone widens, and spreads from the poles, Texans, too, will run increased risks of skin cancers.

Consider also that all across the world, humankind continues to push marginal and formerly wild or semiwild lands into production—prime agricultural lands long ago having been put to the plow. Leaving aside consideration of the loss of biosystem services, as wetlands and rainforest are converted to systems of primary human production (see below under Habitat Modification), and also as increasing numbers of species are lost (see below under Biodiversity), an enormous public health risk is being taken. By now there is little that we can add to the story of AIDS, a pandemic sweeping the world. Virtually everyone, it seems, knows someone who has succumbed to AIDS, whether contracted through sexual transmission, blood infusion, or accident. Yet few people, other than public health specialists, realize that AIDS may very well be the tip of an iceberg. *Many* deadly viruses, lurking in isolated and remote Amazonian or African rainforests, may be released with a vengeance upon encroaching humans. Given international air travel, these humans may, in turn, spread a virus over several continents before realizing that they are infected.

Of course, disease as we know it is itself an artifact of civilization, that is, the concentration of human beings into urban environments. Because of their lifestyles, hunter-gatherers were not susceptible to bacterial and viral plagues until subjected to colonial encroachment—which is one reason that native populations in colonized nations more often fell prey to bacteria than to bullets: they simply lacked immunity to European diseases. Public health experts are extremely concerned about burgeoning human populations jammed into high-density cities that, with the advent of jet travel, offer opportunities for global epidemics. The outbreak of O'nyong nyong fever in Africa in 1959, particularly the rapidity with which it spread, has led epidemiologists to conclude that there are real probabilities (as distinct from possibilities) that a lethal viral plague could sweep the planet, killing as much as 90 percent of the human population.

The point, then, for Texans, is simply that world population does have implications for us. Who knows? South American businesses, providing plywood for the construction of high-rises in Tokyo, pushing the relentless process of development ever deeper into the heart of the Amazon, may represent a real if incalculable health risk to us all.

. . .

Texas is now the second most populous state in the nation, recently moving ahead of New York, trailing only California. As we have noted above, in

1946, at the end of World War II, Texas had 7.2 million people; the city of Dallas had slightly more than 100,000 residents. Today the state has almost 18 million legal residents; the Dallas–Fort Worth metroplex, including Dallas, Tarrant, Collin, and Denton counties, is approaching the 1946 population of the entire state—almost 6 million people—making it the eighth largest SMSA (standard metropolitan statistical area) in the country. Projections of future population growth are yet another matter. Estimates vary from study to study, but a reasonable figure would be 25 to 27 million residents for Texas by 2025.

Clearly, the days are gone when folks from across an entire county would take long wagon rides, two days each direction, just to enjoy each other's company on Independence Day. People were scarce, *then.* Today some Texans think there are too many of us, as we breathe polluted air, live in noisy work and home environments, sit stalled in traffic, and pay increasing property taxes to build the social infrastructure necessary to support "boom times."

The authors believe that most Texans are predisposed to want to be the biggest in all respects, including population. Besides, burgeoning birthrates and the flight of business from the Rust to the Sun Belt have been good for business. Communities love to bill themselves as "growing," and look with dismay, if not horror, on even the possibility that they might lose citizens. City councils routinely approve six-digit expenditures on campaigns to attract new industry. Economists ballyhoo the multiplier effect, meaning that one new job brought to Texas through the relocation of a corporation percolates through the entire regional and even state economy, providing investment opportunities for bankers and developers, contracts for builders and equipment manufacturers, new jobs for carpenters and plumbers.

However, gross population statistics are one thing; the differential distribution of population is another. If Texas is vast, the fact is that most Texans are crowded into a few places. Eighty percent of us live along or east of I-35. More and more of this 80 percent live in two masses of urban-suburban sprawl stretching from Fort Worth to San Antonio on the west and beginning to reach out from Dallas to Galveston on the east. Not long ago these masses did not exist. Now they stretch out and unite once separate towns and cities. Seeing is believing. The maps (Figures 1–6)—to which we will refer again more than once—depict the birth and growth of these Slurbs beginning in 1970, continuing through the present, and projected to 2020. First developed in the 1970s, they have so far proved accurate.

If the spatial effects of population growth are differentially distributed, so are the economic costs and benefits. From a land ethics standpoint such distribution raises questions of land-reform ethics, particularly issues of environmental equity. Federal, state, and regional governments have, for example, broad powers that give them the right of eminent domain. The consequences are that as water reservoirs are built in response to growing urban population, families, even entire communities, are displaced from the land. Such removals are legitimated in the name of the public interest. Justice is ostensibly served, since land owners are paid "fair market value," even when they have no desire to enter into an economic transaction. Often such land taken over by the state has been in a family for generations; it is not an economic commodity so much as a way of life. Variations on this basic theme occur in many other ways. Neighborhoods are cut in half by superhighway projects which bisect them. Homeowners are subjected to intolerable levels of noise because airports must be built or new runways added.

Texas population growth has a hidden, little understood dimension, an aspect that can be illustrated by the concept of an *ecological footprint*: as Texas population grows, the ecological impact of our lifestyles also grows. Which takes us, as we will explain, back to a global perspective. Let's reconsider the almost 6 million people living in the Dallas–Fort Worth metroplex. The wherewithal to support these 6 million souls, living at the relatively high levels of demand of Americans, implies a rippling chain of ecological transactions across not only Texas but virtually *the entire planet*. Scientists (Rees and Wackernagel 1994) have calculated that typical urban areas of industrialized societies require the productive resources of at least ten and possibly twenty times as much land as they physically occupy. Land to grow the beef that we eat, to provide timber products for our houses and paper, to grow cereal grasses for our daily bread and as animal feed, and to provide all the other physical necessities of life. Further, growing populations concentrated in urban areas require water resources from often vast watersheds. Graves' *Goodbye to a River* does not recount a story of the damming of the Brazos to provide water for the small communities and farms that had grown up along its course; to the contrary, it tells a story of dams and reservoirs created to water cities.

Most Texans are unaware of their own ecological footprint. If anything, things seem to be getting better. Texans justifiably pride themselves on the newer, cleaner Texas, partly a consequence of laws like the Clean Air Act, and partly a consequence of initiatives like "Don't Mess with Texas." The authors believe that all this is well and good. But let's push the envelope just a bit further, bearing in mind that we do not claim ecological sainthood for ourselves. We have footprints, too!

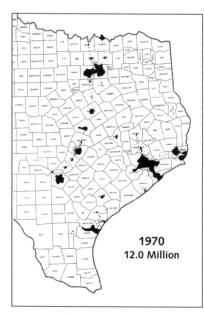

FIGURE 1.
Population Distribution (1970).

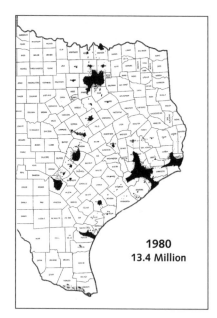

FIGURE 2.
Population Distribution (1980).

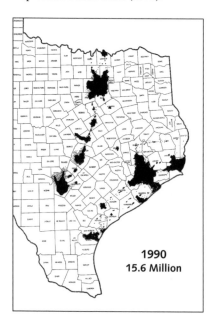

FIGURE 3.
Population Distribution (1990).

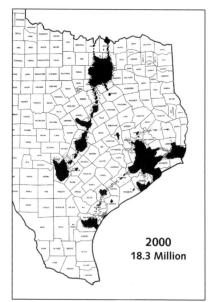

FIGURE 4.
Population Distribution (projected 2000).

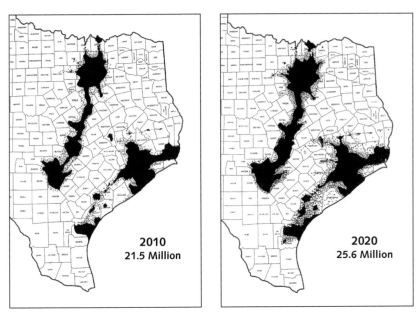

FIGURE 5.
Population Distribution (projected 2010).

FIGURE 6.
Population Distribution (projected 2020).

Consider, for example, all those roads and railroads that make life in the United States and Texas possible, the transportation network that lets us go to and from work or school, that brings tens of thousands of tons of motor and rail freight, including the food that fuels our bodies and the fuels that drive our automobiles and power plants. In 1990, roadways covered approximately 21.5 million acres of land nationally (33,600 square miles, an area slightly larger than the state of Maine) and railroads took up another 7 million acres. On a per capita basis each American's land footprint was 0.086 acres. Extrapolating to Texas (ignoring differential distribution), 1,548,000 acres (2418.75 square miles) of land here have been covered by highways and railroads. In a state as large as Texas, that is slightly less than 1 percent of the land, seemingly an innocuous percentage. Yet consider that the transportation infrastructure, particularly in urban areas, typically covers prime (the best) agricultural land. A lot of good dirt has been covered up. Further, paved areas add enormously to flooding, since water, no longer buffered by the soil's ability to hold it, runs quickly off pavement. Pavement also leads to increased concentrations of pollutants in a variety of ways, including automobile emissions along roadways and toxics downstream.

Consider also a single product, paper. Paper is virtually omnipresent in contemporary life, from cardboard boxes to paper ballots, McDonald's burger containers and grocery store sacks. Again, here is an ecological footprint that is largely out of sight, out of mind. Unlike the forest products used in the construction industry, paper products manufactured from American pulp come from "pulp forests," that is, virtual tree farms, converted to a monoculture of rapidly growing species that are lavishly sprayed with pesticides. A typical North American utilizes about 0.25 ton of paper products per year. Does this seem like a high estimate? Consider that the Sunday paper weighs 5 pounds x 52 Sundays a year. One estimate is that the residents of Texas collectively require 7,200,000 acres (11,250 square miles) of "tree farms" to keep them in paper.

Unlike roads and railroads, which we can see with our own eyes, the ecological footprint for our paper needs is often displaced. American pulp may come from North Carolina or Colorado. But bulk paper also may come from rainforests in South America or Borneo: virtually any place where local price plus transportation cost is less than the market cost of Texas pulp.

By extrapolating this line of reasoning to the multitudes of commodities required to sustain life, we begin to see that the ecological footprint of a typical Texan is very large. In fact, it is roughly like that of the typical American. As 5 percent of the earth's population we Americans consume more than 30 percent of the earth's available resources. (Western Europeans, although slightly more numerous than Americans, consume slightly less, primarily because of more efficient use of energy and recycling.) We purchase quick-food hamburgers made from beef grown in South America on pasture land that was a rainforest inhabited by aborigines less than three years ago, land that will be worthless even for pasture within another three years because of misuse, land that was once home to thousands of species, some now threatened by extinction. We eat mass-produced chickens from Arkansas (where production process wastes poison the water) that were fattened on grain grown in Kansas (where soil erosion is destroying the fertility of the land). We eat nuts and fruits grown in California, where declining water tables are allowing saltwater infiltration from the Pacific, threatening the integrity of the entire Central Valley. We decorate our homes with rugs produced in India by child labor, where indigenous people have been displaced from their traditional lands by World Bank water resource projects, so that the cotton for the rugs could be grown. We burn coal mined in Wyoming, petroleum extracted in Saudi Arabia, and gasoline refined in Bayport. In all cases, out of sight, out of mind.

The point, then, is this: all benefits have a cost. As population increases, ecological footprints grow larger. Ultimately, all ecological and social costs must be paid. Texans, like most Americans of this generation, whatever the degradation of our own local environs, are doing a grand job of passing the note on to other people and other species in other places—and times.

Water. No single issue, it seems to the authors, more aptly characterizes the state of neglect in Texas and dramatizes the need for a land ethic than water. Simply put, without the water provided by the massive federal (and state) water reclamation projects, the Slurbs that sprawl across the eastern part of Texas simply would not be possible. Industry would not have the large quantities of water it requires; neither would private citizens.

Still, the primary user of water in Texas is agriculture. Only 3.2 million people, or roughly 20 percent of the state's population, live in West Texas—here defined as those lands west of I-35. But nearly 45 percent of the state's total water consumption occurs in West Texas: 85 percent of this water is used for agriculture. In turn, most of the supply comes from aquifers—the vast subterranean "lakes" that fuel irrigation agriculture. In part this is a consequence of rainfall or its lack; as noted in Chapter 2, on the eastern boundary of Texas the average rainfall approaches 60 inches per year; on the western edge the average rainfall is about 8 inches.

With the exception of East Texas, our state is best categorized as part of the arid West: the vast Western plains that average less than the 20 inches of rainfall per year required to grow cereal grasses. Little wonder, then, that more than 60 percent of the total supply of Texas water comes from groundwater, that is, from the aquifers that accumulated supplies over aeons of geological time. Texas is blessed with nine major aquifers and nearly twenty smaller ones that, in all, underlie nearly 80 percent of the state. Given its distribution of rainfall, there is little surprise that West Texas accounts for nearly 75 percent of groundwater usage. The eastern regions of the state have supplemented groundwater with a vast system of surface reservoirs.

Due to the state's explosive population growth, the long-term supply of water is uncertain. In this sense, Texas is just like California, only luckier. Southern California experienced massive shortfalls in water supply in the late 1980s and early '90s, due to a confluence of several circumstances—below-average local rainfall and below-average snowfalls in the mountains that feed rivers and reservoirs. But Texas' luck could change. The leaders of today's economies in the Giant Slurbs pay scant thought to the very real possibility of sustained droughts; but Texas has had them before and will have them again.

Water to fuel the Giant Slurbs has already generated its share of controversy, perhaps the best known being that associated with the Edwards Aquifer, which underlies approximately 3,600 square miles of Hill Country Texas. The Edwards Aquifer is the focal point of a 1991 suit filed by the Lone Star Chapter of the Sierra Club in federal court. Growing utilization of the aquifer—then the sole supply of drinking water for San Antonio—by urban and agricultural users meant a diminished flow of water at San Marcos and Comal Springs. One consequence, among others, was the threat of extinction to endangered and threatened species. On February 1, 1993, the federal court (Judge Lucius Bunton's court, Midland, Texas) found in favor of the plaintiffs against the United States Secretary of the Interior. On Friday, June 11, 1993, Governor Richards signed into law a bill passed by the Legislature that regulates pumping from the aquifer—effectively mandating sustainable usage. Such action is unprecedented in Texas. It represents the first time that logic actually prevailed in regulating the pumping of groundwater.

However, no single region west of I-35 better illustrates the Texas water crisis than the High Plains. Since World War II there has been a dramatic, some would say meteoric, explosion of irrigation agriculture there. This system uses powerful water pumps and "pivot systems" to turn groundwater from the Ogallala Aquifer into torrents of profits both for local farm owners and for powerful agribusiness corporations with full-time lobbyists in Austin.

The Ogallala Aquifer is a geological marvel, a vast subterranean reservoir underlying portions of eight states, supporting irrigated agriculture on 15 million acres—one-fifth of the nation's total irrigated cropland—that provide the grain for as much as 40 percent of the fattened beef sent to market each year. Overall, the Ogallala provides 30 percent of all groundwater used for irrigation in the United States. Texas, however, was not a winner in nature's geological lottery. That portion of the Ogallala underlying Nebraska, for example, is ten to twenty times thicker than the layer of water underlying Texas. To compound Texas' bad luck, 80 percent of the annual recharge to the aquifer goes to the portions northwest of Wichita, Kansas—up to 5 inches per year in a wet year. Texas' portion of the Ogallala recharge averages less than a meager 0.1 inch/year. (That is: one inch recharge in ten years!)

Interestingly, Texans are withdrawing water at a rate that compares to Nebraska's. Since the end of World War II Texas' drawdown of the Ogallala is 25 percent. And—another piece of "bad luck"—the Ogallala rests on bedrock containing high quantities of salt and pockets of saltwater; as the aquifer level falls, these salts are pulled up, beginning a process of soil salinization that may destroy fertility even before the water runs out.

It is also ironic that in Nebraska, where the water resource is ample, laws govern the spacing and pumping rates of groundwater wells. Given this system of management, the water resource will last indefinitely, benefiting succeeding generations of human beings and, in this case, disturbing ecology minimally. The case is, regrettably, otherwise on the High Plains of West Texas. As government officials put it, the High Plains are subject to "groundwater overdraft," meaning simply that short-term economic interests are draining the Ogallala as quickly as possible.

If we translate the euphemism "groundwater overdraft" into plain English, it means a system that allows a few individuals and corporations (often absentee owners, headquartered in Houston and Chicago, or even Melbourne and Tokyo) to draw as much water as they see fit from the aquifer with no thought for tomorrow, either ecologically or socially. While estimates vary, at present rates of extraction there are about thirty years of water supply left. Of course, to corporate decision-makers, people who have no neighbors in West Texas, the issue is simply one of extracting the water, turning it into grain, and feeding it to cattle as soon as possible. (We should note that a good bit of the Ogallala water is used to grow cotton, a particularly water-intensive crop.) This is economic alchemy: Water = grain = beef = money. Money that reflects itself on the bottom line; and money that can be invested, elsewhere, in equally or more productive ventures. When the water runs out, the future has been "discounted."

One might think that economic prudence, let alone ecological principles, would dictate public policy which put rates of groundwater extraction into balance with groundwater replenishment. While the state has regulated surface waters (to the consternation of many corporations), groundwater has been nearly sacrosanct. The Texas Legislature has passed two bills that address only a small aspect of our groundwater crisis: as noted above, Senate Bill 1477 regulates pumping from the Edwards Aquifer in order to guarantee minimal flows of springwater at San Marcos and Comal Springs. And Senate Bill 1334 empowers the TNRCC (Texas Natural Resources Conservation Commission) to make and enforce rules governing groundwater quality, but not quantity.

Groundwater issues illustrate another of the simple truths of ecology: everything is more complicated than it seems. Nature is interrelated in ways that defy, time and again, human categorization and schemes.

▪ ▪ ▪

Beyond the supply issue, there is a second aspect: pollution or water quality. Texas is among the national leaders in total discharge of toxics into the water at 36.3 million pounds per year. (See discussion below under Wastes.) Of course, the days are gone when raw sewage was discharged into Texas waterways. The new frontier of toxics lies in the discharge of industrial chemicals. In 1989 alone, the EPA estimated that 5.7 billion pounds (5.7×10^9 pounds!) of toxic substances were released into the American environment (air and water). On that scale, Texas' discharges look relatively modest, only a small portion of the nation's total emissions. That same year, according to American Chemical Society estimates, between 580 million and 2.9 billion tons of hazardous wastes were produced—much of it buried in landfills which may leach into subterranean and surface waters.

Just a few examples of the problem in Texas must suffice. High levels of chlordane have led regulators to forbid fishing along the Trinity River as it flows through Tarrant and Dallas counties. Chemicals (probably originating from the *maquiladora* industries on the Mexican side of the Rio Grande) in river water along the Texas-Mexico border have led to a statistically high number of babies with birth defects (specifically anencephaly and spina bifida). Another Texas water pollution hot spot is Lavaca Bay, located near the middle of the Texas Gulf Coast. At Lavaca Bay, Texas experienced a homegrown version of the infamous outbreak of the 1950s Japanese "Minamata disease"—methyl-mercury contamination that accumulates in the aquatic food chain, primarily fish and shellfish. Human consumers who eat contaminated fish and shellfish suffer neural damage that is either permanently debilitating or fatal. Understandably, the rich Lavaca Bay fishery is closed—a natural resource destroyed, perhaps forever, by thoughtlessness. And all the jobs that went with it. Worse, tidal action appears to be moving Lavaca Bay's mercury-contaminated sediments toward the Gulf and another rich fishery, Matagorda Bay.

Galveston Bay, the nation's seventh largest bay at 600 square miles and its second most productive fishery, is now at risk. More than *60 percent of all wastewater in Texas winds up in the bay,* the end point for more than 750 industrial sources and 560 municipal treatment plants. To compound matters, the nation's largest petrochemical complex is sited there also.

Finally, as upstream users divert water for irrigation and impound water in reservoirs, the sustaining flows of fresh water necessary to maintain the integrity of the aquatic ecosystem is affected—although to what extent is as yet unknown. The ecological effects of water pollution also have social consequences: pollutants don't stay home. The effects of pollutants in Texas rivers are borne disproportionately by those living downstream, such as shrimpers and others along the Gulf Coast. Fish kills and toxic shellfish are just part of the water quality problems facing Texans: the economic consequences for those whose livelihoods depend on shrimping and fishing are devastating. A recent issue of *Texas Shores* (1993) notes: "Three years ago Americans couldn't get enough raw oysters on the half shell. . . . Now hardly anybody wants to eat raw oysters anymore, especially those from Texas."

Habitat Modification. That area of Texas known as the Big Thicket offers one of the best examples on a national scale of an ecosystem—land, plants, animals, water—that was devastated and almost destroyed because of inappropriate land use. We term it habitat devastation on a grand scale. Of course, most of the havoc occurred before Texans even had an idea of an ecosystem, let alone ecosystem management. Today the Big Thicket can be considered one of the bright spots in Texas land ethics, a partially restored ecosystem that, if not ecologically integral, is at least healthy, offering testimony to the resilience of the land community and to good human works. The authors think of the Thicket—at least potentially—as a model land community, where a fair number of citizens are living economically productive lives in ways which are not ecologically destructive. Chapter 6 will offer the details of this story.

Unfortunately, land use across the state generally more resembles the times when the Big Thicket was being devastated than the recent past, when portions of it have been restored. In some ways the late-nineteenth-century plunder of the Thicket, when it was ripped off by sawyers, the early-twentieth-century oil boom, when it was assaulted by wildcatters and the petroleum industry, and the continuing destruction before and after World War II by timber companies, are a microcosm of land use across the entire state. The story varies with biophysical details, but in county after county, bioregion after bioregion, land uses that sometimes catastrophically and often irreversibly modified habitat are well known.

When we think of habitat alteration another of John Graves' books, *Hard Scrabble*, comes to mind. *Hard Scrabble* offers an account of the plunder of the natural largesse of Somervell County over two or three generations by farmers who depleted the land, sometimes bragging that they wore out several farms with their own hands. Pastures were overgrazed, woodlands cut, the soils worn out by cotton cropping. The consequences included massive erosion of topsoils, invasion by exotic plants that displaced prairie grasses and other indigenous species, and general ruin.

Further, as the discussion of Lavaca and Galveston bays implies, habitat modification is just not terrestrial, but aquatic; it includes irreversible changes that destroy wetland ecosystems. In fact, Texas trails only California in wetland devastation, having destroyed 8.4 million acres (compared to 9.2 million for California). Yet Texas remains blessed. It still possesses almost 6 million acres of inland wetlands (80 percent of which are in East Texas bottomlands) and 1.65 million acres of coastal wetlands. Still, the U.S. Fish and Wildlife Service estimates that between the late 1950s and 1980 Texans destroyed 35 percent of their coastal marshes. Since the appearance of the first Europeans within its borders, Texas has lost 50 percent of its coastal wetlands.

But let us return to the High Plains, shifting our focus from water resources to land use: to the ecological consequences of the systems of production on the High Plains. Of course, many residents of Amarillo and Dalhart tend to think that the way things are now is the way that things have always been and always will be. But the land community does not operate on a human time frame: economic, political, or historical.

Over the last ten thousand years, the vast High Plains grasslands supported the southernmost herd (of four) of the buffalo. Associated with the buffalo, the Great Plains' largest animal, were predators, such as the wolf, and a wide variety of smaller creatures, both producers and consumers—collectively constituting a grasslands community. From a strictly biological point of view, plants are the basic life form, determining the makeup of the ecosystem. From one point of view, grasses and herbivores can be described as an ecosystem, but from another grasses antedate the herbivores.

The native grasses of prehistory were well adapted to fluctuations of rain, both seasonal and long-term. In consequence, the prairie soils were not subjected to massive erosion by either water runoff or wind. In those happy times, the natural forces of erosion were in relative balance with forces of soil replenishment—the annual regeneration of the soil through the deaths of plants and the activities of below-ground animals, such as worms and bacteria. The grassland ecosystem, grazed by buffalo, was integral, stable, and to some eyes beautiful.

The recently evolved system, which arose with the coming of Anglos to the High Plains, is in technical terms an *anthropogenic disturbance*. Nineteenth-century buffalo hunters, by eliminating the buffalo (and with them the Native Americans), effectively opened the plains to wave after wave of ranchers and farmers. The last two or three decades of the nineteenth century were the time of cattle empires. Vast ranches, often owned by foreign nationals, dominated the High Plains. Cattle, in one sense, can be said to have replaced the buffalo. But buffalo migrated, effectively precluding the possibility of overgrazing. Cattle do not.

In the last decade or so of the 1800s, severe blizzards and droughts, plus the coming of the barbed wire fence, fundamentally changed land-use patterns. Successive waves of homesteaders settled the southern portions of the Great Plains. Guided by the belief that "rain follows the plow," the immigrants pressed the grasslands into agricultural production. The prairie grasses that had for thousands of years held the fine-grained, sandy soils of the Great Plains were turned under and cereal grasses planted in their place. With the inevitable swing of nature's pendulum, drought returned to the High Plains. But now the grasslands were no more, having been plowed under and brought into a production scheme that yielded profits instead of buffalo. The wind ultimately had its way with the topsoil, carrying it off in vast billowing clouds that, on occasion, reached all the way to Washington, D.C. This catastrophe has been immortalized in American history as the Dust Bowl.

There is no need to recount the details of the Dust Bowl. (Anyone interested could read John Steinbeck's *The Grapes of Wrath*.) The point is that inappropriate land use will ultimately fail, and usually sooner rather than later. The Texas portion of the Great Plains, along with many other areas, was quickly depopulated, with perhaps two-thirds of the residents heading for "greener pastures." Parts of the worst-ravaged areas remain fallow lands to this day, lands taken into federal care as part of the national grasslands system (Rita Blanca Grasslands).

Land management practices changed considerably after the Dust Bowl. But the post–World War II utilization of groundwater again set in motion an unprecedented transformation on the High Plains that represented the apparent triumph of humankind over nature. In the previous section we considered the ecologically disastrous implications of groundwater overdraft. Here we consider that tillage exposes vast areas of West Texas soil to the omnipresent wind. Texas, the land of superlatives, has achieved a number one national ranking in soil erosion (by a margin of more than 100 percent over any other state): an inspiring achievement. The estimated annual loss of 773 million tons of topsoil per year is partly due to the fact that Texas is the largest of the forty-eight contiguous states and subject to near-constant wind as well as torrential rains. Looked at not in terms of total landmass but in terms of erosion per unit area, the Lone Star State loses 14 tons of soil per acre annually. Abysmal land management practices, including clearcutting, lay the soil bare to erosion by natural forces.

One does not have to be an expert to realize that soil, which is produced very, very slowly—on the order of thousands and tens of thousands of years—can be eroded quickly by wind and water. Estimates of topsoil erosion during the Dust Bowl vary, but a loss of 4 inches of topsoil *throughout the region* is a common estimate. In any case, even at the rate of 1/8" per year, 12" of topsoil has an expectancy of only ninety-six years. Whatever the economic rate of return on today's crop, the long-term implications are dismal, since *natural capital* is being used in a nonsustainable way. The use is simply not appropriate to the land, given the nature of soils, winds, and torrential episodic rains.

But habitat modification is not associated only with agriculture on the High Plains or the oil and timber industry in the Big Thicket. Consider the modifications that follow in the wake of the growth of the Giant Slurbs. We have already discussed some of the implications of population growth in terms of the ecological footprint. Perhaps we are now in a position to tie the concept of the ecological footprint to the concept of habitat modification.

Consider that the water reclamation system that has covered the most populous eastern third of the state with reservoirs, has also consumed millions of acres of bottomland, areas of great biological diversity that have provided extremely valuable habitat for a wide variety of mammals, birds, reptiles, and plants. This intensive utilization of surface water has altered the historic flows of fresh water to the Gulf of Mexico, with unknown but potentially catastrophic consequences for aquatic habitat and life. Intensive pumping of groundwater, used to supplement surface water, has produced subsidence along the Gulf Coast, in some areas up to 10 feet, allowing for saltwater infiltration and flooding of subdivisions. Reduced flows from springs fed by underwater aquifers has also led to the drying up of wetlands. Two-thirds of Texas bay shores are eroding at rates of from 2 to 9 feet per year.

Cities such as Austin and Dallas are not located where they are by accident; their locations reflect certain stubborn realities. Like the fact that early settlers needed water for themselves and livestock, fertile soil to grow crops and provide pasture, and woodlots to provide lumber and fuel. There is fine irony in the fact that some of the best land in Texas, in terms of fertility and also in terms of climate, is being consumed by massive urban sprawl.

As authors, we can only pose the question: Is the continued paving over and developing of the richest and most productive lands in Texas in the long-run best interest of the land community? Or does it serve primarily short-term narrowly economic interests?

Biodiversity. Before looking at Texas' own endangered species, let us pull back for a larger view. Globally considered, the earth perches on the precipice of the sixth mass extinction of life (Wilson 1992). Perhaps the best-known previous extinction event occurred at the boundary of the Cretaceous (ca. 63,000,000 BP), when the dinosaurs disappeared in what, biologically considered, was the blink of an eye. However, the extinction event that looms for us is unlike any previous one, since its etiology is anthropogenic: we're doing it.

Not only has humankind initiated an extinction paroxysm, we have also caused the death of birth. That is, we have basically interrupted, on all scales above the micro-organic, the evolutionary processes of speciation. In this sense, humankind has abrogated the power attributed biblically to God. But we, in our actions, are destroyers of life, not creators.

During each of the previous five mass extinctions, simplifications occurred, marked by massive reductions in the diversity of life as well as the complexity of the surviving life forms. This fact causes some scientists to wonder if such a complicated species as *Homo sapiens* can endure, given that the normal run of mass extinction ends up with the highest surviving life form being something on the order of a coyote. Or a beetle.

One frightening analogy for an anthropogenic mass extinction is that of an airplane where, prior to each flight, a few rivets are popped out of the wings and fuselage. The question, of course, is: how many rivets can be popped from the plane before it will crash? The answer is that no one knows. But who would want to fly in an airplane with even a few rivets missing?

The strength of the analogy rests in the notion of the fabric of life: the various life forms on the planet, from tiny flowers in an alpine tundra to three-toed sloths in tropical rainforest, are tied together, to a greater or lesser extent. While relations between alpine and rainforest communities are very weak, in any one community of plants and animals interrelations are very strong. Interestingly, some species are designated as *keystone species*. These species occupy positions of particular importance, being indicators of the ecological integrity of the entire community. In some cases the keystone species is the biological glue that holds the entire ecosystem together.

.   .   .

Texas lacks the biodiversity of an equatorial rainforest, but given its vast size and its diversity of climates, soils, and topographies, it supports an array of life that is nationally rivaled only by California. A very rough inventory, limited to already catalogued species, shows 4,834 species of flowering plants, 247 species of freshwater fishes, 204 species of amphibians and reptiles, 594 confirmed species of birds, and 154 species of mammals. The list can easily be lengthened. Unfortunately, we can also list the factors which undermine this cornucopia: stream channelization, overgrazing, conversion of brush and woodlands to coastal Bermuda grass, the draining and filling of wetlands of every kind, clearcutting, overuse of water resources, the spread and sprawl of urban growth, increasing air and water pollution, and the mushrooming of garbage landfills. This list, too, can be lengthened at will. In every case, both the diversity and the abundance of life are undercut. The biologist has reason for dismay. So do the hunter and the birdwatcher. So, even, in the end, will the Chamber of Commerce.

As noted in the Introduction, the Texas list of "species in trouble" is lengthy, including a large array of birds, mammals, fishes, reptiles, amphibians, and plants—76 species in Big Bend National Park alone.

Air. Day in and day out Texans concerned about air worry primarily about air quality, for obvious reasons of human health. The authors basically approve of these concerns. But the primary threat to Texas involves global climate change.

The air, like the hydrological cycle, illustrates one of the laws of ecology, namely, "Everything is connected to everything else." Texas air is not just Texas air. It has a regional, national, and even global history. One of the most dramatic examples of air that doesn't stay home is acid rain. Fortunately, acid rain has not proven to be a major concern in Texas, though traces of it are turning up in the eastern part of the state, particularly in area ponds and lakes. But Texas faces a variety of serious issues involving the atmosphere, global climate change being the first among these.

The global greenhouse is largely a consequence of carbon dioxide (presently at an average seasonal concentration of 345 ppm in the atmosphere). Other greenhouse gases include methane, or CH_4 (1.6 ppm), and carbon monoxide, or CO (0.1 ppm). All greenhouse gases contribute to climate change through climate warming; carbon dioxide is especially important because of its direct involvement in the so-called global carbon cycle. Figure 7 is a simple model of the global carbon cycle. The model contains estimates of the contribution of each "compartment"—that is, atmosphere, oceans (including carbonate sediments), terrestrial biomass (such as rainforests), and soils and fossil fuels—to the carbon cycle on a yearly basis. The agro-industrial contribution is small in relation to the contributions from other sources. However, this small anthropogenic contribution has upset the historically established mean.

Particularly relevant to Texans in considering the implications of global climate change is that portion of the carbon cycle influenced by the utilization of hydrocarbons (fossil fuels). Prior to the scientific and industrial

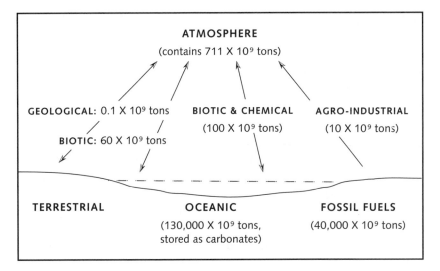

FIGURE 7. The Global Carbon Cycle (adapted from Odum 1993). Forecasts from the IPCC (Intergovernmental Panel on Climate Change) confirm that a relatively small amount of carbon dioxide from human activities has major effects on climate.

revolutions, the carbon cycle had achieved relative balance (since the end of the Würm glaciation). However, since industrialization, global CO_2 has risen, at first slowly, then rapidly since World War II. Anthropogenic inputs of carbon dioxide into the atmosphere exceed the rate at which it can be removed either by the growth of vegetation, or by the oceans' carbonate system. Table 1 shows the rise in atmospheric concentration of CO_2 for the last century.

In total, humankind has increased the amount of atmospheric CO_2 by 25 percent in the last century and more than doubled the level of CH_4. (Methane is the result of incomplete or anaerobic decomposition of organic matter which, in the atmosphere, is oxidized to carbon dioxide. The primary sources of methane are natural: wetlands, termites, and agriculture, especially the production of rice and cattle.)

Climate warming is one hypothesized effect *of increasing atmospheric concentrations of CO_2.* Increased carbon dioxide creates what is called the "greenhouse effect" by reflecting longwave radiation from the earth back to earth, retarding the dissipation of heat into space. Major consequences of climate warming include rise in sea level, and changes in both climate patterns (for example, distribution and frequency of rain) and the habitation patterns of plants and animals. A mean temperature rise of 1° to 4° Celsius (about 2° to 7° Fahrenheit) would melt polar ice and rapidly increase sea level. UNEP (United Nations Environment Program) estimates that a 1-meter rise in sea level would displace one-quarter of the world's population (in excess of one billion people). A 3° Celsius rise (approximately 5–6° F) would raise sea level by 2 meters (slightly more than 6 feet).

Even though climate warming remains uncertain in the strictest sense, the overwhelming consensus of expert scientific opinion, including the National Academy of Sciences (U.S.A.) and the Royal Society of England, supports the precautionary principle, recommending that humankind collectively act in the near future to reduce those activities, such as the production of carbon dioxide and the destruction of rainforests, that contribute to the possibility of irreversible environmental change. A 1988 NASA (National Aeronautics and Space Administration) project confirms that global temperature over the last century has risen, just as predicted by several climate models. And satellite telemetry now provides proof positive that sea level is rising: 0.25 inch in the last two years. The Intergovernmental Panel on Climate Change (essentially a consensus body drawing together the expertise of twenty-five hundred climatologists) concludes that anthropogenic climate warming is already underway.

Major consequences can be anticipated for the state of Texas in either the case that a global protocol on climate change is established or that it is not. Texas, for example, is *numero uno* in the country in terms of CO_2 emissions—1.67 million tons per day. (Another way of putting it is to note that we produce more CO_2 than Canada or Italy.) The competition for this dubious honor is stiff, since the United States is the world's leading producer of greenhouse gases. Obviously, the Texas economy is heavily involved in processes that produce these gases. As the world becomes more attentive to this problem, fundamental changes appear to be in the making. A policy on global warming that mandates reduction in carbon dioxide emissions would have major socioeconomic effects in the Lone Star

TABLE 1. *Atmospheric CO_2 Concentrations*

Year	Atmospheric CO_2 Concentration
1890	est. 290 ppm
1958	315 ppm (yearly mean, measured at Mauna Loa)
1990	345 ppm

State. Similarly, the predicted 1-meter (approximately 3 feet) rise in sea level that would follow in the absence of a policy on global warming would adversely affect Texas ecosystems and populations along the Gulf Coast. (Imagine, for example, the effect on Galveston Island.) Changes in jet streams could effect massive changes in historical patterns of rainfall distribution and frequency; several climate models predict a shift in the temperate belt to the north. The IPCC forecasts increased rainfall and food production in northern North America and reduced rainfall and food production in southern North America, including Texas and the Midwestern grain belt. The implications of this massive shift are almost unthinkable, both in terms of economic disruption and human suffering.

Waste. Waste divides itself into many subcategories, from the prosaic (household garbage, used washing machines) to the exotic (toxic byproducts from industrial processes). Another useful distinction marks off those which are hazardous (toxic chemicals, raw sewage, radioactive materials) from those which are not (waste paper products). Even "benign wastes" can be problems, in terms of landfill, use of natural resources, and other factors. Texas produces more solid municipal waste per capita than any other state: 5.6 pounds per person per day compared to 4.3 pounds nationally.

As stated previously, the authors have no illusion of providing either a definitive or exhaustive statement on waste. Our treatment of waste, as with the other categories, is framed by land ethics, primarily land-use ethics. We should note, also, that recent developments, such as market incentives for recycling and the emerging science of industrial ecology, give us some reason to think that Texans, along with other citizens across the country, are beginning to take some waste problems seriously. Nationally, approximately 1.5 million tons of lead-acid batteries (primarily car batteries) are recycled each year, nearly 90 percent of the supply needed for new batteries; similarly, 55 percent of the aluminum for soft drink cans, 45 percent of the cardboard for corrugated boxes, and 33 percent of the paper for newspapers come from recycled materials. Estimates are that approximately 80 percent of the 20 million tons of municipal waste generated annually could be recycled. The Omnibus Recycling Bill (passed by the 72nd Texas Legislature) mandated the goal of 40 percent recycling by 1994. That percentage has not yet been reached.

On the other hand, the United States still has no scientifically validated procedure for the disposal of radioactive wastes. West Texas not only serves as a repository for radioactive wastes (primarily at the Pantex plant, about 17 miles northeast of Amarillo), but it continues to attract radioactive waste storage "entrepreneurs," who propose that the low population and "wasteland" characteristics of the Trans-Pecos region make it an ideal site. The authors wonder, "ideal for what?" There are no known safe methods for the storage of radioactive wastes. What gives us reason to think that the United States could protect such repositories for tens of thousands of years when the Egyptian dynasty could not protect its pyramids from plunder for more than a few centuries? (It should also be noted that Department of Energy officials have been repeatedly sued by Texas citizens for withholding information on proposed radioactive waste facilities.)

The actual management of hazardous wastes from nuclear power plants gives further reason for concern. The AEC (Atomic Energy Commission) has been faced with several near catastrophes, like Three Mile Island, despite manuals and procedures deemed to be fail-safe. There is no reason to think that nuclear facilities in Texas are any exception. For example, TU Electric has been repeatedly cited for hazardous operation of its Comanche Peak power plant. TU Electric was recently fined $50,000 by the NRC (Nuclear Regulatory Commission) for the release of 24,000 gallons of radioactive water into the Brazos River. The NRC (Kessler 1993) notes concern about these events "because they were caused by a combination of inattention to design control requirements, a failure to use established procedures . . . , a lack of control of licensed activities by shift supervision, poor communications between shift personnel (and) poor decisions by the very personnel that TU Electric was relying upon to improve field activities." (The DOE Pantex facility also underwent an "emergency" in August 1993, when nearly 100,000 gallons of water flooded six weapon bays.)

Globally, waste poses enormous problems. The floor of the North Sea, as the world learned recently, has been the junkyard for decommissioned Soviet nuclear vessels. More generally, the world's oceans continue to be repositories for literally hundreds of thousands of tons of waste products, from human body parts and used hypodermic needles to toxic chemicals and raw sewage.

In terms of land-reform ethics the authors are particularly concerned that the hazardous wastes generated by all the day-in-day-out activities of industrial society tend to have adverse differential impacts on specific segments of the Texas land community and associated human populations (Bullard 1990; Goldsteen 1993). Regrettably, as with CO_2 emissions and soil erosion, Texas leads the nation in the total volume of toxic chemicals either produced or transferred during manufacture. Superlatives do not end there: the Monsanto plant at Alvin produces the largest amount of waste of any single plant in the nation!

Again, as with the biodiversity issue, all of us face great uncertainty and equally great risk (Colborn, Dumanoski, and Peterson 1996). Of approximately 65,000 industrial chemicals now in use, scientific study has been undertaken on only about 650 (< 1 percent). Which means that 64,000 chemicals (what are a few hundreds among friends?) used in the present industrial economy have unknown toxic effects on living organisms: not only on humans, but on plants and animals. To further complicate matters, virtually nothing is known about the interactive effects of toxic chemicals in rivers or in the air. Similarly, what is known about the persistency of these chemicals once released into the air or the water? the rate at which they accumulate in plants and animals? the levels at which accumulation becomes hazardous to health? And so on.

Effectively, the "better living through modern chemistry" rhetoric (popularized by E. I. Dupont Co. in the 1950s and '60s) turns out to be much like the rivets analogy discussed above. We simply do not know what we are doing. And hazardous wastes compound biodiversity issues, since no present life forms on the planet evolved in environments containing any of the 65,000 human-made chemicals.

Perhaps we could learn from the "primitive life forms" contained in pond water, creatures that swim toward nutrients (yummy, yummy) and immediately turn tail when toxics are introduced into their microworld. Texans should be so smart. In 1989, Texas industry collectively poured 793 million pounds of chemical toxicants—the weight of 320,000 automobiles—into Texas water and air. We are number one in this category by a margin of almost 100 percent. The existence of thirty Superfund sites in the state suggests that all is not well here in toxic waste regulation.

The Need for a Texas Land Ethic

How did Texas come to its state of neglect? What explains the pervasiveness of our land crisis, in all its many guises? There are a variety of explanations. We might believe, for example, that Texans are a bunch of mean-spirited miscreants and criminals, barely one step ahead of the law, bent on harvesting, mining, cutting, and otherwise consuming anything to which they hold "clear title." Let posterity fend for itself, and the devil take the hindmost. This explanation, however, has several negative consequences. For one, on this hypothesis, a statutory framework that criminalizes certain kinds of behaviors is necessary. For another, it presents a dour, even cynical, view of human beings.

Another possible explanation is that Texans simply haven't known any better. Unlike the previous hypothesis, this conjecture is relatively "high-minded," resting on the ancient assumption that ignorance is the cause of evil (in this case, the abuse of the land), and that environmental education, more than anything else, can lead to changed behaviors. This theory has always seemed incredibly naive, even from the time of Socrates, who first suggested it. There are always those, not necessarily the minority, who stand to profit from the plunder of the commons, regardless of the public good.

This dilemma is the much discussed "tragedy of the commons," elaborated by Garrett Hardin (1968). Two centuries ago the "commons" referred to land that a community used for grazing livestock—a system where no one had exclusive right to its use. In today's context, the term is applied to air, water, and other biosystem services. As with the commons of yesteryear, no one owns the air and the water. Predictably, much as common land was the first to be grazed in old times, so the commons are systematically exploited and degraded today. Because of *the appearance* that no one has an economic interest in maintaining the commons, individuals and firms use air and water as free goods in order to avoid the costs of proper waste disposal.

A third explanation is that the political economy of a market society makes environmentally sensitive business behaviors financially prohibitive, especially in the absence of a framework that regulates an entire industry (including foreign competitors). This hypothesis is enormously skeptical as well, since it implies that there are no solutions to ecological dysfunctions until some radical changes or restructuring of the political economy occurs: in short, an ecologically sustainable society will require a political revolution. The authors place no great faith in either the possibility of a revolution or the likelihood of a positive outcome of one. We tend to believe that, despite the economic power of corporations in control of the mass media and electoral politics, there is still some vigor in democratic life, some possibility of renewal from within. But discussion of those possibilities would entail authoring a different book.

Thus we come to a fourth explanation, one that does not point the finger of blame at unsocialized agents of eco-destruction, claim that ecological education can turn the tide of destruction, or believe that revolution is in the offing. Rather, it appeals to a deceptively simple formula: the total human effect upon the land is the consequence of three factors. Namely, the total population, the level of demand placed by the population on the environment for goods, and the technology employed to do so. $E_{total} = P \times D \times T$ (Population x Demand x Technology).

The equation suggests that ecosystem effects, such as depletion of stratospheric ozone, are a function of the demand for refrigeration, air conditioning, aerosol propellants, and so on, the size of the human population making such demands, and the technologies (primarily technologies employing CFC_{12} and CFC_{13}) used to manufacture the commodities and services that meet the demand.

Clearly, the equation is not analytically robust; the harder you push it the less useful it becomes for purposes of analysis. No single unit of measure for E_{total} can be defined. It's at best an "intuitive" amalgam of a variety of measures, such as extinction rates, soil erosion, climate warming, thinning of stratospheric ozone, water toxicity, and so on. On the right-hand side of the equation, things *appear* to be more discrete; in truth they are not. Even ignoring the question of how P, T, and D interact, the single measures alone are problematic. Population projections (P) are based on linear models which are notoriously inaccurate and highly conjectural. Demand (D) takes us into the domain of economics and economic welfare. We might quantify D, very roughly, in terms of GDP (Gross Domestic Product), although a welfare economist would never accept that. T or technology has no measure per se, unless we restrict it to a single quantity, like kilowatts consumed. And then it reflects D more than T.

Nevertheless, the equation is a useful device for summarizing our discussion of the state of neglect. A recent report by the National Commission on the Environment (1993) observes:

> Over the next 50 years—within the lifetimes of many of us and of all our children—economic activity in the United States is projected to quadruple and global population [P] to double at least. If growth of this magnitude occurs with current industrial processes [T], agricultural methods [T], and consumer practices [D], the results could be both environmentally [E_{total}] and economically disastrous.

The fact that Texas' land community is in a state of neglect is itself evidence that the powerful of our state—both private interests and government—inhabit a timeworn worldview, fashioned in an unecological age, that views the earth as little more than dead, inert matter subject to human appropriation. From this perspective, the land community is valueless until humanized, that is, categorized for utilization in the economic scheme of things, developed, and used to sustain human civilization. From this perspective, there can never be too many Texans nor any limit to demand: if Texans need to change anything, it is simply the technology that we use to exploit the raw materials provided by nature.

This perspective is based on an illusion.

Lorrie Coterill, President,
Groups Allied to Stop Pollution
(GASP), South Dallas
County Landfill.

4

LAND ETHICS AND ECONOMICS

We are not economists. The analysis offered here is directed toward ecologically concerned citizens, not economists. Setting out from the previous chapters, we extend land ethics to economics, since there is an apparent opposition between them. This chapter offers answers to *a few* of the many questions which lie at the interface of ecology and ethics with economics. We are under no illusion that we offer final answers. Whole books would be required to flesh out the detail of the issues discussed here. Even then, formidable problems of uncertainty would remain. (Uncertainty comes both from the complexity of ecosystems and cultural systems themselves and from the limitations of theories of risk.)

Lies, Damn Lies, and Economic Statistics

Of one thing we are relatively sure: Any economic theory which legitimates ecological abuse of the land finally leads to ruin, regardless of "economically successful" short-term outcomes or "technological innovations" (smokestack scrubbers, "water-efficient" cereal grasses, "fuel-efficient" automobiles). The state of neglect (see Chapter 3) implies that regardless of the perceived manifestations of Progress, such as profits made, high-rise buildings constructed, new industries attracted, population growth, new jobs generated, and low-priced consumer commodities, ecological reality is different.

Farming practices that exhaust aquifers and expose the soil to erosion, transportation systems that generate greenhouse gases that alter the global carbon cycle, manufacturing processes that emit toxics into the air and water, human reproductive rates that sustain exponential population growth, and water resource projects that deny adequate inputs of fresh water into tidal estuaries and saltwater bays are, whatever our intentions and regardless of our perceptions, a sure path to environmental degradation.

No Texan needs a Ph.D. in either economics or ecology to realize that the human economy *and* nature's economy are vitally interlinked: from the sun, which delivers the energy that drives photosynthesis, to biophysical processes like the carbon cycle, to the evolutionary process itself. Yet mainstream economics, in the United States and Texas, usually fails— or flatly refuses—to recognize the interconnections between the human economy and nature's own.

One way of approaching this difficulty is to examine a few of the statistical measures used by economists to assess economic performance. These are primarily the GNP (gross national product), the rate of economic growth (growth of the GNP), and per capita income. Judged by the GNP and its associated measures, the United States generally, and the many states individually, are economic success stories. These statistics undergird the American dream of prospering. So long as the GNP grows—the story goes—Americans are much better off.

Even a cursory review of the American economy, from the turn of the century through the present, appears to confirm that the dream has come true! Though the rate of economic growth has varied from year to year, the trend throughout the century has been upward. Economic statistics paint a rosy picture, blemished only by cycles of inflation and recession, so-called stagflation, a single Great Depression, and a stubborn problem of income distribution, that is, of an apparently permanent underclass. Some 10 percent of Americans own 90 percent of our real wealth; the richest 1 percent own 35 percent. Only one other democratic society in the world—India— has such a large economic differential between its wealthiest citizens and those in the bottom third.

However, given the focus of our argument, we must leave aside questions of environmental and economic justice, since these issues go beyond the strict confines of a land-use ethic. Table 2 offers a statistical record of GNP and per capita income from 1950 through 1990 (based on C. W. Cobb 1989). The data apparently show that America is getting bigger and better. At least we all seem to be getting richer, having twice as much per capita income as we had a mere forty years ago. If this rate of increase is ex-

TABLE 2. *GNP and Per Capita Income (in Constant 1972 Dollars)*

	1950	1960	1970	1980	1990 (est.)
GNP (billions)	534.8	737.2	1,085.6	1,475.0	2,100.00
Per capita income	3,512	4,080	5,294	6,477	7,000

trapolated ahead two centuries, each and every American will enjoy nearly a quarter of a million dollars of income each year (in 1972 dollars). Not quite as rich as Ross Perot and Lamar Hunt, but close.

Yet the GNP and per capita income are measures that ignore the ecological realities of sustainable life. We are like the farmer who consumes the seed corn necessary for next year's crop or a lawyer who burns casebooks to keep warm in winter. Our present economic success is predicated on the utilization of natural capital. Natural capital, as we use the term, includes biophysical processes, such as the carbon cycle, nonrenewable resources, such as fossil fuels, and so-called renewable resources, like timber. Standard economic theory categorizes natural capital as raw material.

We agree with mainstream economics that natural capital (raw material) is necessary to build civilization, including the food we eat, the homes and buildings where we live, work, and go to school, the roads on which we drive, the sanitary systems that flush away our wastes. Economists use the term *man-made capital* to refer to those things human enterprise has created out of natural capital. We see no problem in this definition, nor in the utilization of natural capital to build civilization. There is no alternative.

We believe that mainstream economics fails, however, in at least two places. One is in its assumption that the processes by which natural capital is converted into man-made capital can go on without limits. The hard fact is that nature's economy does have limits (Georgescu-Roegen 1971; Hardin 1993). The other lies in the assumption (*the substitutability function*) that man-made capital and natural capital are substitutes rather than complements. On this rationale, for example, there is no reason to worry about consuming the natural capital of the Ogallala Aquifer, because man-made capital can be substituted for it. By utilizing the Ogallala we create wealth, which in turn—the story goes—can be invested in fusion energy facilities used to desalinate water from the Gulf of Mexico and pump it to the High Plains.

Ignoring the extreme optimism regarding technological fixes reflected in this view (the discovery of knowledge cannot be predicted; the availability of fusion energy remains an enormous uncertainty), the substitutability assumption fails at the level of common sense. (We are here following the arguments of Daly 1994.) If man-made capital is substitutable for natural capital, then the opposite should be true as well. But if natural capital could be substituted for man-made capital, then there would have been no reason to build a human economy. Further, man-made capital requires natural capital, regardless of the substitutability assumption. Facilities to desalinate saltwater and distribute fresh water cannot be built out of economic smoke and mirrors. They require cement, sand, steel rebar for reinforcement, wood for frames, water for cooling, exotic metals and alloys for the fusion furnace, cast iron pipes by the hundreds of miles for distribution, and so on.

Fortunately, other statistical measures—ones that reflect the realities of life on earth—exist. One of these is the Index of Sustainable Economic Welfare (ISEW), which incorporates a number of ecological variables: costs of air and water pollution, species extinction, lost wetlands, topsoil erosion, and degraded fisheries, all of which are excluded from national income accounts. Proponents of the ISEW refuse to include clear losses (of natural resources) as gains. Incredibly, such losses, no matter how catastrophic, are counted as pluses to swell the GNP. To take only one example, in conventional economics air pollution is supposed to be an economic benefit rather than a cost, since it creates industries and jobs designed to clean up the air. On such assumptions, if Texas were to lose the entire petrochemical industry around Galveston Bay through some natural catastrophe, the billions of dollars lost would be added to the GNP for the year in which the disaster took place!

Unfortunately, although the ISEW has ecological and moral standing, it is not yet widely known. In terms of the policies and procedures of the federal government, particularly those that affect the nation's economy, the ISEW may as well not exist. The Council of Economic Advisors, to cite only one instance, employs only conventional statistical methods in making recommendations.

Ecologically considered, the ISEW gives a more accurate picture of economic well-being than the GNP. For example, under traditional measures, it is rational to clearcut old-growth forest, as demand permits. But such an accounting of value is enormously truncated, that is, restricted to one-time, short-term economic values gained from the timber sale. Other values, such as recreation and tourism, ecosystem services (prevention of soil erosion, habitat for endangered species), and aesthetic and cultural values, such as beauty and a commitment to preserving at least some wilderness areas, are ignored.

Table 3 shows how economic performance looks when ecologically relevant measures are incorporated into statistical aggregates (based on C. W. Cobb 1989). Per capita ISEW, we note, equals GNP minus the Ecological Costs (EC) divided by population (P):

$$\frac{GNP - EC}{P} = ISEW$$

The ISEW also measures costs such as commuting, urbanization, and other psychological variables that we do not include here.

Clearly, the picture in Table 2 must be modified. Though per capita income (Table 2) nearly doubled in forty years, per capita ISEW made only modest gains through the 1970s. *Since then there has been a decline.* Which suggests, among other things, that the human economy, as presently organized, has reached a point of diminishing returns in relation to nature's economy. In the next chapter we make some concrete suggestions about how this decline might be reversed. By attending to the fact that nature's economy and the human economy are closely coupled, we could accomplish what has been termed an economic "about face." Namely, embracing the concept that man-made capital and natural capital are not substitutes but complements.

TABLE 3. *Index of Sustainable Economic Welfare (in Dollars)*

	1950	1960	1970	1980	1990 (est.)
Water pollution (billions)	-9.0	-11.5	-14.9	-15.3	-16.0
Air pollution (billions)	-25.2	-25.1	-30.0	-24.3	-20.0
Wetlands loss (billions)	-10.0	-13.6	-17.2	-19.5	-21.0
Farmlands loss (billions)	-7.2	-13.7	-20.9	-28.6	-35.0
Depletion of nonrenewables (billions)	-20.6	-25.5	-30.9	-74.5	-60.0
Environmental damage (billions)	-84.0	-116.2	-161.8	-223.0	-270.0
Per capita ISEW	2,488	3,052	3,723	3,672	3,300

We emphasize that the ISEW is not the Holy Grail of ecologically informed economic statistics. For one thing, it is a relatively conservative measure. Ecological amenities, such as the biosystem services provided by the global carbon cycle, are in some aspects "priceless." No substitution can be made, at any price. The use of any economic statistic entails an assumptive framework. But how is depletion of nonrenewable natural resources priced? Clearly, even more conservative approaches than the ISEW can be envisioned. But, regardless of insufficiencies, the ISEW is a step in the right direction.

It is the height of arrogance to believe that human beings could even engineer, let alone provide the financial resources to implement, an ameliorative (substitute) technology for biosystem services. Consider the carbon cycle. Imagine the sucking sound (to steal a phrase from Ross Perot) of an imaginary machine as it pulled carbon dioxide from the atmosphere in order to head off climate warming. Thus, the proposal that we price air pollution (for example, increasing CO_2 concentrations) is dubious; many ecological economists believe that it is impossible. Typically air pollution is priced—if it is priced at all—in measures of human illness (respiratory infections, lung cancer, and so on), lost wages, damages to buildings and homes, and damages to crops. A similar pricing problem exists in relation to the depletion of natural capital, such as topsoil generated over hundreds of thousands and fossil fuels created over millions of years. Technological optimists tell us not to worry, since as costs increase, marketplace incentives will see to the problem of substitutes. Such talk is not reassuring, given the twentieth-century track record of technological innovations gone awry.

Though they are imperfect, such measures as the ISEW are essential to putting a land ethic to work, and thus restraining the growth-at-any-cost dynamic that is driving nature's economy downhill. Ecological economists sometimes distinguish between marginal utility (exchange value) and total utility (use value) in order to show the limits of prices. Consider diamonds and water (see Daly 1994). At the margin, diamonds are of high value and water low. Yet the total utility of water is incalculable, an absolute necessity, while the total utility of diamonds is minimal. As the situation on the High Plains clearly illustrates, water, which has low marginal utility, can be converted into money because its total utility, that is, its irreplaceable function in agriculture, is high. Once water is converted into money, through the alchemy of agribusiness, it can be used to purchase diamonds.

In the early years of economics, which, not surprisingly, corresponded with the beginnings of the industrial revolution, economists were able to ignore the effects of industry on air, water, soils, resources. Such effects could easily be written off as "externalities." There were fewer people then, comparatively abundant resources, and a much less developed industrial system. By the end of the Second World War the situation had changed radically. Vastly expanded human populations, a massively productive and messy industrial system, and correspondingly reduced resources—as Leopold saw so clearly at the time—painted a radically different picture. Most economists, however, continued to hold the notion that natural "externalities" could be ignored. They reasoned and computed as if nature were only real when priced by the market: as if it existed only for the sake of, and as an infinite resource for, human economics.

Clearly, this will not do. The world we live in is not dependent on the market; the market, and everything else humankind does, are dependent on the world. An exemplary question, in the comparison of Tables 2 and 3, is therefore this: "Should . . . marginal utility exchange value be used in evaluating those parts of the hydrologic cycle outside the human economy, or for deciding whether to further expand the frontiers of the exchange economy?" (Daly 1991). That is (to strip away the jargon), should the prices achieved in the market be used to evaluate the processes of nature upon which the market itself depends? The answer is clearly no. The market is useful. But it is not a god which designs nature according to its whims.

This simple realization—not a radical theory, but, in fact, the soul of common sense—has so far failed to sink in. There is little realization of it in economic practice, and minimal ethical awareness of the results. If you own the land, and prefer short-term profit (i.e., maximizing exchange value) over long-run sustainability (optimizing total utility), then by all means pump the Ogallala dry. Clearly, the prehistoric waters captured in the Ogallala have exchange value only when brought into the human economy. The more pumped, consistent with the needs of the crops grown, the greater the return. The problem is that maximizing short-run utility bankrupts the system, that is, destroys the total utility of the Ogallala. So which would you rather have when the Ogallala has been exhausted? A second chance on ecologically sustainable and economically rational utilization of the resource? Or diamonds?

Another way of putting the issue is this: Who decides? What constituencies actually make land-use decisions? If you are an executive working for a multinational agribusiness conglomerate headquartered in Houston or Chicago or Tokyo, your decision is going to be made on the basis of short-term economic rationality. Similarly, if you are a local resident whose income is dependent upon running the pumps and tractors for that same agribusiness firm, you will likely opt for pumping the aquifer dry. But if you are a stake-holder in the High Plains culture, someone who has dug in and taken root, a person with a name and a face that knows his or her neighbors, someone who has children and would like them to remain part of the community, then things look different. Short-term profit maximization is, in fact, inimical to your way of life.

We have used the example of the Ogallala Aquifer several times. But it is not the only one. Just sticking to the example of underground water, there are several others. The Hueco Basin and the Mesilla Basin near El Paso are being "mined," leaving that metropolis with increasingly saline water and an uneasy future of water scarcity. The Trinity Aquifer in the Dallas–Fort Worth area (and elsewhere) has also been mined, with resulting falls in water levels of 100 feet or more. Most economists would probably duck the embarrassment of having to treat such losses as gains. But precious few of them would bother to include these costs at all in their accounts of civic profits and losses. But the losses are economically as real here as on the High Plains. In all such cases faulty economics leads to the destruction of resources that could have lasted indefinitely.

Economic Imperialism

William Smart offers a classic definition of Economic Imperialism: "The economic goal of civilization is to turn the whole natural environment of man from a relation of hostility or indifference into a relation of utility" (quoted in Daly 1991).

Historically considered, Texas is, if not an unqualified success story, at least well down the road toward the triumph of humans over nature. The early settlers had to displace hostile elements, primarily the various tribes of the Na Dene, the Native Americans, who already lived here. Along with the "redskins," a few other hostile factors, like wolves and mountain lions, hawks and rattlesnakes, wetlands and deserts, had to be conquered, too.

With the aid of modern technology, Texans have also turned formerly indifferent elements of nature, like water and raw land, to useful economic service. With modern drilling, formerly "indifferent" reservoirs of oil, like those contained in the Austin Chalk, have yielded black gold. Fueled by population growth, the prairie land in the northern parts of Dallas County, which grew cotton before World War II, has been covered with high-priced residential and commercial real estate developments. And the subterranean reservoirs of countless aquifers have been brought to the surface and turned the semiarid plains into an agricultural oasis.

Economic Imperialism rests on a cluster of notions centering on the idea that human beings are somehow above or outside nature, able to control it through the power of science and its offshoot, technology. This philosophy drives the relentless conversion of natural capital, in all its diverse manifestations—wilderness, waters, fossil fuels, forests, flora, and fauna—into civilization. Ernst Mayr (1982) writes that "it was a tragedy both for biology and for mankind that the currently prevailing framework of our social and political ideas developed and was adopted when the thinking of Western [civilization] was largely dominated by the ideas of the scientific revolution, that is, by a set of ideas based on the principles of the physical sciences."

The consequence is that the belief that nature is valueless until humanized goes intellectually unchallenged and institutionally empowered in a system that literally consumes nature. Hence the bulldozing and concreting of our creeks, without regard for either the animals and plants that once lived there, or for the people living downstream, whose homes will now flood more quickly and more often. Hence the draining and/or filling of countless wetlands, often unnecessarily, almost as a kind of afterthought. (Texas has managed to rid itself of 60 percent of its inland wetlands and 50 percent of its coastal wetlands in this way.) Hence the headlong assault on East Texas forests around the turn of the last century: a "mining" operation which left little more than forests of stumps in its wake, over vast areas of the Woodlands. Only Economic Imperialism could have justified such heedless assaults. Nor is it yet acceptable to suggest an alternative. Any countervailing narrative, such as the ecological idea that nature is not so much a resource as a living system upon which human existence fundamentally depends, a living system whose health is intrinsically bound with the health of our culture, remains today at best a minority report from the far margins of society. Obviously, we think this needs changing.

Marketplace Theory

Marketplace theory—which functions to cement Economic Imperialism in place—rests on the assumption that prices reflect the optimum social situation, where supply and demand are relatively in balance, and where competition has winnowed out the inefficient producers so that consumers enjoy the best possible goods at the lowest possible prices. Further, on this theory nothing stands outside the market; thus land and clean air and water are all things which, in principle, can be priced. Even environmental policy can be, indeed, should be, determined through the market.

By asking citizens "How much would you pay for clear air?" or "How much would you pay to ensure that your children had adequate supplies of water?," such "resources" will be properly priced. Accordingly, air and water and all other resources will be put to their highest and best use, so that the greatest good for the greatest number of stakeholders in the market society will be the outcome.

The problems with the marketplace as the sole determinant of land use are many, although defenders of the market ideology claim that the market can redress virtually all ills. However, we believe that there are at least four problems with the marketplace.

First, marketplace economics is based on the notion that land is nothing more than raw material, essentially valueless until humanized. What is land worth? What somebody will pay for it, as the old story goes. In other words, land is valueless until it is brought into the human scheme of things, the market itself, where buyers and sellers establish its worth. The idea that an East Texas old-growth forest, for example, has an enormous ecological value that outstrips its market value is unthinkable on these grounds. (That, in turn, helps explain why there is so little of this forest left.)

Recently a new discipline, ecological economics, has attempted to include environmental costs and benefits in the economic calculus. We agree that this is an important step in the right direction, and that it can lead both to more accurate accounting and better policy decisions. Among the achievements of ecological economists is the development of the notion of *biosystem services*: the function of a swamp in cleaning up water pollution, of birds in limiting insect populations, of coastal marsh in providing spawning grounds for fish and shellfish. It is true—and important—that up to a point dollar figures can be given for such services. We doubt, however, that the market can ever take account of many of the most important of these services. What is the value of the biosystem services provided by the old-growth forest, such as providing habitat for endangered species, converting CO_2 into oxygen, fixing carbon in woody and leaf mass, holding topsoils in place, and allowing rainwater to slowly percolate into waterways rather than run off in a soil-eroding torrent (not to mention values such as human recreation)?

Our very lives depend on clean air and ample supplies of water, relatively stable climates and patterns of rainfall, fertile topsoils and insects to fertilize our orchards, and all the thousands of amenities, including medicines from natural plants, provided by nature. But if land, construed broadly as including the plant and animal communities, is only raw material, valueless until brought within the rubric of the marketplace, then the prospect for nature is dire. For the earth and the biosystem services offered by nature are doomed: they have value or worth only in an exchange system. The consequence is the modern economic imperative—that is, the conversion of the land to standing reserve, to raw material serving only as fuel for the economy. Holes in the ozone, exhaustion of aquifers, extinction of species, erosion of soil, the destruction of habitat, and the prospect of global climate heating are the inevitable aftermath.

A second difficulty with marketplace theory is its unexamined assumption that prices, as set by supply and demand, can address questions of *throughput*: of the sheer possible scale of economic activity. The question is simply "How much is enough?" The market answers: "There can never be enough." The dynamic process that converts raw material into the goods and services demanded by consumers knows no limits: either economic or biophysical.

The implicit assumption is that human beings could never have enough material things to sate their appetite. We call this the "greedy little pig" theory of human beings. No distinction between the quantity of life and the quality of life operates, according to this viewpoint. Progress is assumed, by definition, to consist of nothing more than the steady increase in per capita standard of living. (The psychological reality is that most middle class Americans enjoy rising standards of living, yet report declining satisfaction with life.)

If the greedy little pig theory (GLP) is true, all failure to be greedy is "irrational." So those families on the beach at Galveston or Corpus Christi, sitting quietly watching the surf or tossing a softball or just talking to each other are considered by GLP theorists to have missed the mark. They should be downtown, their faces greedily pressed to storefront windows, scoping out the consumable wonders within; or, if rational, they should be out working to be able to buy such wonders. (After all, if they made enough money they could afford to go to a classy resort—and sit on the beach.) One wonders why, if humans are inherently greedy without remainder, so much effort has to be put into advertising—to stimulate buying and to reinvigorate the (innate?) desire to work overtime. If greed is the whole truth, it ought to be more than self-sufficient.

What is required, in order to offset this marketplace theory, is some concept of economic sufficiency. Economic sufficiency primarily involves the notion that those things which give the deepest, even ultimate, value and meaning to human existence have nothing to do with the quantity of life, once the quantity of life is adequate to the satisfaction of basic needs for food, shelter, clothing, health, education, and so on. And by extension, economic sufficiency also involves the idea that the relentless pursuit of growth in material standards can actually undercut the quality of life.

This leads to the third problem with marketplace theory: the status of "externalities" and the assault on the "commons." Externalities are, in the broadest sense, real results that are not taken account of by the market (and are thus "external" to it). We breathe the air, warm ourselves in the sun, use rivers as sources for drinking water, and hope the rains will revive the prairies after a hot spell. All such factors are for mainstream economists externalities. Collectively, these are the "commons": goods common to all but owned by none. Air, rain, river water, sunshine, a stable climate make up the commons, which we all use and rely on without cost.

The problem is that though marketplace theory does not take account of these factors, using them does have costs. Waters used as "sinks" for garbage and sewage become polluted, spreading disease and making their reuse impossible. Similarly, air, when polluted, creates bad health and damages crops and buildings. Eventually, and reluctantly, economists may begin to work such factors into their equations. But for the most part they prefer to ignore them. The rest of us, however, have to live in this world.

Our transportation system provides a vivid example of the failure of marketplace theory to take account of the real costs of externalities. Fossil fuels burned in transportation provide 18 percent of the global load of carbon dioxide. The Union of Concerned Scientists estimates the actual costs of each gallon of fuel in environmental risk and degradation at $2.53. A little arithmetic suggests that this cost can mount up quickly. Texans use 9 billion gallons of gasoline every year for transportation—second only to California at 13 billion. Multiplying through (9 billion times $2.53) we get 22.77 billion dollars per year of costs which traditional economists do not consider at all. Costs in damaged lungs, allergic reactions, skin problems, crop damage, loss of work. Costs in Dallas, Victoria, Longview, El Paso. Here, too, there is, we admit, room for debate. The 22.77-billion-dollar figure is certainly not set in concrete. We would like to believe it is too high. But can anyone doubt that, in terms of air pollution alone, our transportation system has real and serious costs?

Such costs, which, again, do not appear in the equations of market theorists, are of only one kind. There are many others. Many towns and cities abuse the commons by emptying their wastes, not fully treated, into rivers. Downstream users (Gulf fishing and recreation industries) pay the costs. Toxic waste dumps and derelict oil storage tanks and pipelines take their toll on natural environment and human health. Eventually the external becomes internalized, and the public picks up the tab.

The fourth problem is the tendency of marketplace theory to downplay environmental costs or even to deny them outright—which clearly has its effects on policy-making. It leads to our making decisions with slight realization of what the effects will be. One of us recently flew from Dallas to Houston and back—in August. When we were boys or even young men the Texas skies were relatively clear, wonderfully blue, even on hot summer days. Now a haze of pollution hangs over the landscape from Dallas to Houston, horizon to horizon from the air: an atmosphere-deep layer of photochemical smog now so commonplace that many do not realize that it is human-made and historically new. In winter the pollution haze is more dispersed. Yet in the mornings it hangs in a gauzy rust-colored sheath over urban centers, blown away gradually by the morning winds, only to form again by night.

The truth is that no one computed the costs of this new phenomenon or tried to foresee it. Prevailing attitudes made this unlikely, if not impossible.

But besides this general tendency, there are some particular flaws in marketplace theory which influence decision-making. One is called the Environmental Impact Hypothesis: the thesis that in curbing pollution or limiting clearcutting or reigning in the breakneck exhaustion of natural resources, we destroy the economy on which we depend. We will deal with this thesis independently, in the following section.

The Environmental Impact Hypothesis

Some Texans have begun to wonder if there is not some way that economy and ecology can be brought into a complementary relationship, so that "economic development and progress" do not lead to ecological disaster. They wonder if there is not some way that Texas can restructure itself so that we do not lead the nation in all the wrong categories and trail in the right ones.

By emphasizing the integrity, stability, and beauty of the land community, land ethics call into question the notion that the marketplace can determine the highest and best use (and even the idea that marketplace economics determines the most efficient use). Such an idea takes us into terra incognita. As Leopold noted, society succumbs to the fallacy of economic determinism, the belief that the market can and should determine all land use. If land ethics hold that something more than the market might determine our relations to the land community, we face several questions. What would a Texas land ethic mean in economic terms? Does it mean that utopian preservationists and misanthropic conservationists would dominate the political economy, so that more and more land would be locked up in "no trespassing zones," where no human would ever go? or that water reservoirs necessary to sustain continued demographic and industrial growth would not be built? or that air quality laws would be enforced so stringently that the Texas petrochemical industry would be "run out of town on a rail"? Does it mean that the Texas economy itself would wither on the vine, stagnant at best and likely dwindling away to nothing?

The answer to these questions is generally this: good ecology is good economics. The dominant ideology and the Texas tradition is that nature is there to use. Thus, environmental regulations, however noble in their intent to guarantee clean air and water or to protect endangered species, wetlands, and so on, are economically ruinous. This conjecture is known as the Environmental Impact Hypothesis (EIH). But in fact, environmental regulation has not adversely affected either the American economy or the Texas economy. Let's look at the EIH in more detail. (We are following the analysis of Meyer 1992, 1993.)

The first premise of the EIH is that environmental regulation constrains overall economic performance. That is, as environmental regulation increases, the costs of compliance become increasingly burdensome, even onerous. Additional staff are hired, increasing labor costs; environmental impact studies have to be made, introducing delays in production schedules; records have to be kept and reports made, increasing the paperwork overhead; expensive changes in production processes are necessary to comply with new standards for emissions, and so on. The end result is increased costs of doing business that adversely affect prosperity.

The second premise is that environmental regulation suppresses growth in employment. Again, the argument is relatively simple. As regulation increases, constraints on emissions, land use, and so on increase costs in all industries and, in cases of resource extraction, may either preclude development or add onerous production and restoration costs. As costs increase, profit declines, and thus capital for investment in either new or expanded productive enterprise, and perforce jobs for people, declines. Manufacturers delay investment in new facilities. And, as consumers become increasingly insecure about their own employment they delay or forgo expenditures on consumer products and housing, further exacerbating economic downturn.

The third premise of the EIH is that environmental regulation diminishes productivity and undermines competitiveness. The arguments here are somewhat more complex. One argument is similar to that in the first premise above: that increased costs of doing business diminish profit, and thereby the capital necessary to invest in scientific research and development (R&D). Thus obsolete processes of and facilities for manufacturing stay online and overall productivity declines. A second argument involves the psychology of corporate executives, who are schooled in "minimizing risks" and "maximizing profits." Thus the cycle of innovation is short-circuited, since new products and technologies represent unknown present, and worse, future, environmental consequences. "Safe products" that have met existing regulations represent the lowest risk and expectation of highest return.

The fourth premise is that environmental regulation drives industry to states or nations with less stringent or no environmental regulation. The argument is predicated on the idea that when the costs of doing business in one place are greater than the costs of doing business elsewhere, including the costs associated with relocating, then industry must move.

The primary prediction based on the EIH is that those states with the weakest environmental regulations will enjoy relatively greater economic prosperity than those states making strong efforts to protect environmental quality. One piece of intensive research, called the Meyer-MIT study, based on data from 1982 through 1989, reviewed the economic performance and statutory framework of all fifty states. This time frame coincided almost exactly with the Reagan era, which saw a massive rollback in federal environmental initiatives and funding. Otherwise known as the New Federalism, the Reagan era essentially extended the opportunity to each state to follow its own bliss. Some, such as Oregon, California, and Hawaii, continued and even improved the statutory and administrative framework concerning environmental quality. Others, such as Louisiana, New Mexico, and Utah, cut back.

This study showed that the protection of environmental quality did not undercut economic prosperity as measured by conventional economic indicators, including gross state product (GSP), total (nonfarm) employment, construction employment, manufacturing productivity, and overall labor productivity. Not only did those states with the strongest environmental policies not experience adverse economic consequences, they either economically outperformed those states with weaker environmental regulations or, at worst, experienced neither gain nor loss. Of course, the conclusion cannot be drawn that environmental regulation is the *cause* of economic prosperity. The results, however, were surprising—even to those who did the report. A recent update of the report shows the same trends continuing.

Generally, states which legislatively and administratively pursue environmental quality are also states that invest heavily in social infrastructure:

education, scientific R&D, transportation, communication, and all the other factors that help create robust economies. There is also evidence that states that invest in infrastructure are those that attract the industries that will dominate the twenty-first century—"high tech" industries in computers and electronics, communications, education, medicine, and so on. Scientific R&D and skilled labor forces are an absolute necessity for such industry. And environmental regulation encourages R&D—so-called industrial ecology—that fuels product innovations and economic savings in materials, energy use, waste disposal, and input-output efficiencies (doing more with less). Chapter 5, which considers the feasibility of putting land ethics to work, looks at industrial ecology in some detail. Environmental efficiency in industry can actually make, not cost, money.

Where does Texas figure into this analytical scheme? Given the overview in Chapter 3, the answer is obvious. In terms of environmental regulation and enforcement, the Lone Star State is very near the bottom, edged out for that dubious distinction by Alaska and Louisiana (states whose economies remain even more heavily dependent on natural resource extraction than our own). With an economy still based in large measure on the utilization of natural resources, from subterranean water and the soil to timber, gas, and oil, Texas is a state where "environmental regulation" is a dirty word to most spokesmen for the economy.

Some Stray Reflections

An attentive reader of this chapter will find two currents of thought, juxtaposed. The first is a plea for an economics which, insofar as it deals with costs and benefits—insofar as it puts a price on things—spells out those costs in full. It cannot be repeated too often: an economy that wrecks its ecology wrecks itself. Environmental costs must be "internalized," whether these are ecological costs pure and simple or human costs, in the diminished quality and value of life. The second (often implicit in our discussion) is an insistence that life cannot be wholly reduced to dollars, cannot be measured in quantities.

Some will argue that we cannot have it both ways; that is, we cannot argue for accurate quantities while warning that not all phenomena can be understood in quantitative terms. This would be true (that is, a contradiction) if we believed the economic viewpoint is the only valid viewpoint. Of course, we do not. Mark Sagoff's statement (1988) of the issue is unsurpassed: "Our environmental goals—cleaner air and water, the preservation of wilderness and wildlife, and the like—are not to be construed, then, simply as personal wants or preferences; they are not interests to be 'priced' by market or by cost-benefit analysis, but are views or beliefs that may find their way, as public values, into legislation." Once we realize that environmentalism cannot be adequately conceptualized in terms of the market and consumer willingness to pay for clean air, wilderness refuges, or the protection of endangered species, then the possibility of reconsidering economics in terms of land ethics (or other ethical and religious schemes) becomes possible (see Oelschlaeger 1994).

That is, we do not concede that a dollar figure can be placed on every aspect of the world. (How much, for example, would you be willing to sell your son or daughter for? The answer is that they are priceless.) But insofar as we have to deal with costs, benefits, jobs, industries (and we certainly have to), we should spell out the whole cost of what we do, and stop sweeping environmental costs under the rug.

A 160-acre uranium mill tailings pond in Karnes County. Contents: six million tons of radioactive waste and chemical solvents.

5

ARE LAND ETHICS PRACTICAL?

Our concern at this juncture is with the issue of practicality. Assuming that the analysis to this point has persuaded the reader, the question is: How can we get from where we are now, in an ever worsening land crisis, to where we might like to be, that is, enjoying prosperous lives of value and meaning amid local, national, and global ecosystems that are ecologically sound? More specifically, can land ethics be institutionalized within the prevailing political economy?

The Skeptics' Case

Skeptics claim that land ethics are impractical, especially for Texans involved in the real business of providing the goods and services that keep the economy going. Some might go further, arguing that the authors are looking at the world through rose-colored glasses, a view typical of people who never had to make a payroll, service the debt on land or machinery, or actually get things done.

Some of the skeptics' arguments cannot be dismissed out of hand. Consider a Texas ranching family, especially one that does not own its land free and clear. We recall the story of the rancher who inherited a million dollars. Asked what she was going to do, she said, "Run cows, 'til the money runs out." Which is to say the hours are long, the risk great, and profits uncertain, even in the best of times. The last thing a rancher wants to hear is that there is an endangered forb on the northeast quarter that is now off-limits to grazing. Or that groundwater use is going to be curtailed, so that the section planted in maize has to be cut back to a half-section. Or that concern for soil erosion requires the land be left in permanent cover. Land ethics talk in the college classroom is one thing. But it won't make the mortgage payment.

Similarly, urban dwellers have grounds for skepticism. Even if persuaded to adopt the land ethic, what are they to do about population growth? About endangered species? About air and water pollution? While citizens may dislike the bad effects of urban growth, they typically feel they have little or no say with the state legislature or the Chamber of Commerce. Similarly, the city council is more concerned with the effects of economic growth, like increasing crime rates and the need for additional infrastructure, than with plans to moderate or even stop it. Even worse, land ethics, as evident in the concern for clean air and water, greenbelts and parks, and wetlands preservation, appear to some citizens to offer little more than hikes in the cost of living for environmental amenities that they have little time to enjoy. Concern for the integrity, stability, and perhaps most of all the beauty of the land community seems awfully expensive and, frankly, impractical.

The skeptic could also argue that business corporations, even sole proprietorships, also face difficulties in practicing land ethics. Imagine—the argument might go—that a Fortune 500 CEO decides to institutionalize land ethics through raw materials procurement that alleviates risk in shipment, through production processes that employ state of the art pollution control and energy-efficient technologies, and through marketing strategies that encourage conservation. In a competitive environment, such policies would almost immediately begin to affect the corporation's reason-to-be, the bottom line. Perhaps the quarterly statement would not show the difference, but the annual report would. This hypothetical corporate executive would soon be circulating a résumé to "head hunters" and job placement firms. We do not accept this scenario as it stands. Many businesses do make a serious effort to protect the environment and do succeed in turning a profit. But it is a common argument against "green" economics. And it does make a certain amount of sense. Not every attempt to do business while protecting the environment can succeed. Not, at any rate, under present circumstances.

Turning the Rhetorical Tables

The immediate rejoinder to skepticism is the counter-question: Is continuing upon the present path practical? Texas is locked in the grip of a land crisis that promises to get worse and not better. Despite its many economic merits, how can a system that is damaging global, national, and bioregional ecology be considered practical in the long run? A strong economy cannot be built on faulty ecology. Practicality, as it turns out, is not a transparently clear concept; it has many dimensions that our cultural and individual calculus of preference and value omits.

There is a famous essay by Charles Lamb which describes a farmer anxious to eat pork. In his haste, he ushers a pig into his barn and burns it down around the hapless creature. Not only is this not an inspiring tale of kindness to animals, it is a parable of how not to do economics. The problem here is not with the end of the activity: to satisfy hunger. The problem is that *the means* are irrational. Which is to say impractical.

Consider agriculture, although manufacturing could do as well. Farming practices that lay the soil bare, subjecting it to the forces of wind and water erosion—to the extent that Texas leads the nation in soil erosion— are irrational. Water utilization that promises to drain the Ogallala Aquifer by 2025, destroying the Panhandle economy with it, is irrational. A food industry that expends tens of thousands of calories of energy producing and transporting a 350-calorie microwave dinner to the supermarket is irrational. Subsidies that encourage farmers to plow every field to the fence row to produce a grain surplus that requires subsidy money for storage are irrational.

Paying the lowest possible cost for food is economically rational, so long as economic rationality is confined to the short term. However, when we realize that store prices reflect only a portion of the true costs, our notion of economic rationality begins to change. Agriculture in its present form is designed to turn soil, water, and energy derived from hydrocarbons into food, as quickly and as profitably as possible. The difficulty with the system is that it is simply not sustainable: it will collapse as the consequence of its "economic success," that is, from soil erosion, the exhaustion of water supply, and the collapse of nonrenewable energy (and fertilizer) supplies. Of course, these costs will largely fall on our children and theirs. They will disproportionately bear the costs of our folly.

One can imagine similar examples in all the factors that define our lives: manufacturing, transportation, housing, energy, water—the entire economy, writ large. What is the practicality, we wonder, of creating Giant

Slurbs from San Antonio to the Red River? What is the practicality of petrochemical plants that pour their poisons into Lavaca Bay? What is the practicality of a system of private transportation that, beyond its energy inefficiency and pollution costs, encourages population growth and suburban sprawl?

In the long run, judged over time frames of decades, even centuries, the present economy is patently impractical: a zero-sum, lose-lose game. But there are alternatives—real alternatives that avoid the mind-numbing abstractness and complexity of economic theory. The following section offers some principles and examples of a green economy.

What Is a Green Economy? Principles and Examples

Just prior to the UN Conference on Environment and Development (UNCED), held in Rio de Janeiro (June 3–14, 1992), the World Council on Business and Development (WCBD) issued a report, edited by Stephan Schmidheiny, entitled *Changing Course* (1992). The report has come in for considerable criticism, some deserved and some not. The WCBD, we note, was constituted almost entirely of the business elite of the world—the CEOs of multinational corporations comprising virtually an "international Fortune 500."

Thus, the report of the WCBD (also known as the Schmidheiny report) is not a document prepared by the Austin Chapter of the Sierra Club or a master environmental plan produced by the engineers at TNRCC (Texas Natural Resource Conservation Commission). The WCBD states that global society is not sustainable: reform is necessary. *Changing Course* acknowledges that the present industrial paradigm has not only created enormous and widening gaps between the developed and developing nations, but has done so in a way that is rending the ecological fabric of the planet.

We endorse the message of the WCBD. But we have difficulty with the envisioned alternative to business as usual; namely, sustainable development. We believe that the WCBD does not take seriously the question of limits, such as the carrying capacity of the earth, and thus overemphasizes the possibility for continued economic growth as measured in conventional terms. We also believe that the WCBD places too much faith in technological fixes.

No doubt, *Changing Course* has direct implications for corporations in Texas: they, too, are part of the global skein of business and manufacturing. Interestingly, during the same time frame as the UNCED at Rio and the deliberations of the WCBD, more than fifty of the largest corporations doing business in Texas came together for a meeting on air quality and manufacturing processes. They concluded that Texas has serious air quality problems. Understandably so, since more than 50 percent of Texans breathe air that does not meet federal standards (see Chapter 2). Recognizing that air pollution is a spillover from manufacturing, these corporate leaders resolved that they would voluntarily reduce atmospheric emissions by more than 50 percent by the year 2000.

Some critics believe that the public pronouncements of the WCBD are no more than a global public relations campaign. They argue that *Changing Course* sabotaged binding resolutions, consideration of which was pending at the Rio Conference, that would have established international regulation of multinational corporations. Texas environmentalists, similarly, are skeptical that our own local polluters will significantly change their behavior, even if required by law to do so. For one thing, critics believe that any corporation existing in a competitive environment can neither afford to cease and desist from the exploitation of the commons nor to invest in alternative technology.

Our immediate objectives preclude pursuing such questions. We want to emphasize the recognition by the WCBD—unquestionably the most authoritative body of international business leaders ever assembled—and by Texas business leaders, of the necessity to change business as usual. The motives of these parties are another issue. But further argument should be over the kind, scale, and pace of change and the means by which such change can be institutionalized.

■　■　■

What are the principles that underlie a green economy, that is, an economy that among other virtues is consistent with a land ethic? There are a wide variety of proposals, some of which, like the Brundtland Report (the popular name given to the report of the World Commission on Environment and Development, published under the title *Our Common Future* in 1987), are controversial. Whatever its insufficiencies, *Our Common Future* deserves credit as a catalyst for the conversation concerning *sustainable development* (roughly defined as economic growth that ameliorates poverty without compromising the ability of future generations to meet their needs). The *Rio Declaration on Environment and Development* (1992), otherwise known as *Agenda 21*, represents a modest improvement over the Brundtland Report. Crucially, this document was signed by 178 nations, including the United States plus all the other industrial democracies of the world. Though we do not entirely agree with the principles set forth in

Agenda 21, they are at least a step in a practical direction. Interpreted through the frame of land ethics, so that the intrinsic value of the land community is recognized, *Agenda 21* represents a long stride forward.

What are the principles of the Rio Declaration? Altogether there are twenty-seven; fortunately, a dozen, as we interpret them, constitute the core of a green economy (United Nations 1992). These are:

1. Human beings are entitled to a healthy and productive life in harmony with nature; thus, human beings are recognized as members of a land community, and their rights to a fully human existence are balanced with the rights of nature. Human rights are not, in other words, absolute, but contextualized by a surrounding land community. To take an example close to home, the interests of Austin real estate developers should be balanced with the rights of the golden-cheeked warbler—or the Edwards Plateau Aquifer—to continued existence. It would also make a good deal of sense if the goals of Austin and San Antonio real estate developers were balanced with the needs of Barton, Comal, and San Marcos springs, including the rare, scarce, and endangered species that live there, and the people who enjoy their clear, abundant waters.

2. The economy should equitably meet material and ecological needs of present *and future* generations. So viewed, questions of both temporal and spatial scale are central to economic development. To apply the principle to Texas, the short-term interests of agricultural and industrial water users should be balanced with the long-term maintenance of water resources. It is patently unjust to pass the costs of mismanagement to future generations. The same is true of the soils that sustain agriculture. Farming and ranching practices that cost the Lone Star State an average loss of 14 tons of soil per acre per year are not exactly a gift to our children and our great-grandchildren. Every effort—including the volunteer efforts of landowners and land managers—should be made to slow such irrecoverable losses.

3. Environmental protection is an integral part of economic development and cannot be considered apart from it. In the context of this chapter, this principle underscores the notion that institutionalizing land ethics is not only practical, but necessary to the creation of a sustainable economy. Gulf Coast petrochemical plants that poison the water and destroy fisheries are economically impractical, to understate the situation. Gulf Coast urban and real estate development that destroys valuable salt marsh is as short-sighted as, in the end, it is economically costly.

4. All nations must cooperate in conserving and restoring the integrity of global ecosystems; developed states and nations bear a larger responsibility, since they place the greatest burden upon the planet. So viewed, a green

economy recognizes the reality of our ecological footprint. Thus, in light of the all too real possibility of global climate warming, Texans bear special responsibility to reduce CO_2 emissions. One way is to promote the use of natural gas, instead of petroleum, as a basic fuel. As in so many other cases of possible workable reform, this one languishes, though its value to the natural gas–rich Lone Star State is obvious. Another way is to persist in working with Mexico not only in containing the massive sewage and toxic waste effluents poured into the Rio Grande, but to attempt to salvage enough remaining wild areas on both sides to preserve a remnant of the native plants and animals. Such efforts have begun; but a real, continuing effort must be made to sustain them.

5. All societies should reduce and eliminate unsustainable patterns of production *and* consumption *and* promote appropriate demographic policies. To locate the mass of Texas' population in the eastern or east-central part of the state, to encourage massive doubling and redoubling of population, is to court both social and environmental misery. The resulting problem is twofold: vast populations encouraged to settle in one region; and in that region an unchecked tendency toward sheer sprawl, with attendant loss of farmland, forest, and prairie, an explosion of road building and increased nonpoint pollution, and the expectation of a lowering quality of life. If we have stressed the problems posed by the Giant Slurbs in this book, it is not because we enjoy doing so. The size of the ecological footprint created by this mindless sprawl appears ominous to us. Texas must, to cite only one possible response, seriously entertain questions that address the advisability of its open border policies. Perhaps Rust Belt corporations ought to stay in the Rust Belt.

6. Environmental decision-making entails broad-based participation; states should make information widely available and guarantee access to judicial and administrative proceedings. This principle is so revolutionary that it actually recommends the practice of democracy. Thus, to take an example, Panhandle citizens should be given what they have never had in regard to Pantex: honest and complete information and the binding right to decide for themselves if they want radioactive waste in their backyard. For another example, Texas TV stations should interrupt their dismal cavalcade of murder, robbery, wreck, and fire on the evening news with brief discussions of environmental problems and options in local areas. We concede that this is a dangerous and frightening idea. It might change civilization as we know it.

7. States should enact effective environmental legislation. This principle, in combination with number 6, would put an end to the republic of

special interests that not only subverts environmental policy-making but bends environmental law to selfish economic interests. For example, Texas might assume the responsibility for implementing the gasoline tax recommended by the National Commission on the Environment (see Getting the Price Right, below). (Principle 7, obviously, is a necessary means to the institutionalization of other principles.) We suggest also that legislation be enacted to make it easier, for those private citizens so inclined, to donate greenbelt land along creeks and rivers (see Chapter 6). Since many Texans hesitate to donate land to governmental bodies, receiving and protecting of stream corridors could be the province of either organizations like The Nature Conservancy and the Natural Areas Protection Association, or other independent organizations.

8. States should prevent the relocation of hazardous materials and manufacturing processes that cause environmental degradation and/or impair human health. This principle would foreclose the possibility of ecological disasters such as the one occurring at Bhopal, India. Union Carbide located its petrochemical plant there because environmental regulations prevented siting the plant in the United States and other developed nations. To take an example nearer to home, Pantex would cease to be a repository for radioactive materials and substances from other states or from the federal government. Whether low-level nuclear wastes should be disposed of in Hudspeth County (in Trans-Pecos Texas) is certainly debatable.

9. Environmental impact assessments should be used to evaluate proposed activities that affect the environment. This principle would prevent such disasters as the near extinction of our national symbol, the American eagle, by DDT. To consider Texas, had an environmental impact assessment been conducted, the chemical plant that is destroying the Lavaca Bay fishery through mercury pollution would not have received approval to do business.

10. States shall monitor and notify other states of potential transboundary environmental effects. This principle would encourage compliance with principle 4, above: namely, there is but a single planetary ecosystem. Thus, everything goes somewhere, and very often that somewhere is tens, hundreds, or thousands of miles away. To take an example close to home, had Mexico acted on the basis of this principle, Texas mothers would not have been exposed to poisoned water and air along the Texas-Mexico border, and babies without brains would not have been born to these mothers.

11. States shall develop laws regarding corporate liability and compensation for the victims of pollution and other environmental damage. This principle, if enacted into law, would extend the precedent established in

the case of the *Exxon Valdez*. Although litigation is still being conducted, the Exxon Corporation has been fined more than $1 billion and has spent more than $500 million on cleanup and restoration. In the Texas context, this principle means that polluters and other environmental abusers, including municipalities, must pay. If this principle were enforced, the petrochemical industry of Harris, Galveston, and other Gulf Coast counties would necessarily find new, less polluting production technologies. So would industries a lot farther inland. We wonder whether the slipshod, hazardous use of insecticides in the Lower Rio Grande Valley and elsewhere would continue if corporate liability and personal compensation legislation were explicit and strict.

12. Last, but not least, the precautionary principle: Where there are threats of either serious or irreversible environmental damage, scientific uncertainty will not be used to delay implementation of cost-effective measures to preserve ecological integrity. This principle has been roundly ignored during the last fifteen years: the Clinton-Gore administration has been little better than the Reagan-Bush and Bush-Quayle administrations. Our nation and state continue to act as if there were no coming day of ecological reckoning. As E. O. Wilson recently noted in Atlanta, at the 1994 meeting of the prestigious American Association for the Advancement of Science, environmental degradation deceives us because of the nature of change. Once critical thresholds are passed, collapse can be catastrophically sudden. Again, to take a Texas example, the Panhandle economy appears to be humming along as usual. But as the bottom of the "water barrel" nears, the collapse of the regional economy—which will ripple across the entire state—may be precipitous.

■ ■ ■

Lists are useful, perhaps, for purposes of instruction and information. Clearly, these twelve principles are worthy of our consideration: if acted on, they could lead us toward a green economy. Even better, perhaps, is the blueprint for a green economy proposed by Paul Hawken, himself a businessman, in his best-selling book, *The Ecology of Commerce* (1993). At the least, Hawken's book is a good read. *Agenda 21* (the Rio Declaration) reads like any document produced by bureaucrats. It is boring and tedious. Hawken is exciting.

Hawken's ideas, we emphasize at the outset, are consistent with the twelve principles outlined above and with a market economy—at least one that internalizes ecological costs. The essence of the ecology of commerce is this: viable commerce must be based on ecological principles. Which, on

Hawken's analysis, is precisely the problem with our current economy: it flies in the face of ecology.

Like UNCED, Hawken offers lists of objectives that lead toward a green economics. More important, in our opinion, is his thesis that a green economy can be built by imitating the basic principles of nature's own. The human economy, whatever its short-run success, is fated for a speedy end. It simply is not sustainable over even the intermediate haul of a few decades or centuries, let alone several millennia. But nature gives us an example of an economy that has been successful for tens of millions of years.

How then does nature operate? And what specifically is the business corporation to do? Hawken simplifies answers drawn from the emerging field of industrial ecology, offering his readers a relatively accessible discussion, as compared to the intimidating nature of scientific discourse. On his account, nature operates in terms of cycles, that is, circular processes that function as closed loops. Minor perturbations in these processes are regulated through positive and negative feedback. Fueled by the renewing inputs of solar energy, a natural process consists of closely coupled, living loops, integrated in ways that ensure the continuation of the process.

One of the keys that Hawken emphasizes is waste. Nothing is waste in nature. Everything goes somewhere, continually utilized in ongoing biological-ecological processes. No organism or community produces toxic byproducts that degrade other organisms or communities. All the elements and chemicals upon which life depends are caught up in continuous cycles. Of course, over hundreds of thousands or millions of years, as the geological record confirms, there can be significant changes in, for example, the carbon cycle. The earth's atmosphere was once almost entirely devoid of oxygen; green plants irreversibly altered its composition, taking carbon dioxide from and adding oxygen to the atmosphere. But the norm is a relative constancy that, barring the impacts of meteors or massive volcanic eruptions, is conducive to the replication of life.

Further, greed is absent in nature. The lion and the tiger, the hawk and the falcon, kill only what they can eat. And they do so in ways that do not degrade their prey: by taking the old, lame, and sick, predators enhance the genetic fitness of the populations on which they themselves are dependent. It is the wolf, Leopold observes, that has shaped the sinews and muscles that propel the deer's flight. Nature appears to be regulated through a system of checks and balances; if predators grow too numerous, the availability of prey diminishes, controlling the predator population. If the rains are ample, predator and prey both flourish. If drought occurs, predator and prey populations both diminish.

In contrast, Hawken explains, human-created systems operate in ways that directly contravene natural processes. For one thing, our production-consumption processes are linear rather than cyclical. We produce massive amounts of waste in production and consumption. The chemical industry, for example, has created more than sixty-five thousand artificial substances that played no part in evolution: they are not part of nature's cycle. The consequence is a forgone conclusion: these substances, whatever their economic utility, are unraveling the fabric of life. Even ostensibly benign products, from disposable diapers to automobile tires, are problematic, since they are not biodegradable: they accumulate in prodigious proportions as waste. (We cannot forbear from noting the wonderful exuberance of Texas in this respect. If all the solid waste generated in one year here were stacked up, it would form a wall 21 feet high and 21 feet wide from Houston to El Paso. Let's call it the Great Wall of Trash.) Further, many technologies, such as the internal combustion engine, are both engineering marvels and ecological problems, upsetting the natural cycles that govern the composition of the atmosphere: in consequence, billions of tons of greenhouse gas are altering the composition of the earth's atmosphere. Finally, to compound the problem, unlike the dynamic interrelation of predator and prey, there is no feedback system to check human population growth. As Paul Ehrlich, one of the world's leading demographers and author of *The Population Bomb* (1968), recently noted (Ehrlich and Ehrlich 1990), the population bomb is no longer hypothetical: it has exploded. Unlike any other species, we grow unchecked, literally covering the face of the planet.

What's the solution? Hawken (1993) answers: "We need to imagine a prosperous commercial culture that is so intelligently designed and constructed that it mimics nature at every step, a symbiosis of company and customer and ecology." Step one might be replacing energy derived from hydrocarbons with solar energy, the fuel that has driven life on earth for more than 3 billion years. Is it necessary to point out that the Lone Star State has plenty of sunlight? Step two might be doing more with less. Hawken suggests that we reduce consumption of energy and natural resources by 80 percent within the next fifty years. This, he contends, "is not as difficult as it sounds. In material terms, it amounts to making things last twice as long with about half the resources."

Notwithstanding the proposal by the WCBD (1992), on Hawken's account today's corporation is like a "junkie," caught up in a self-defeating cycle of addiction and short-term pleasure (profit). But addicts can kick the habit, beginning with the self-critical realization that they are addicts.

So viewed, the Schmidheiny report is the first step on the part of an international business community: the admission that today's corporations are addicts, hooked on short-term satisfaction that is proving corrosive in the long term. Business enterprises, Hawken (1993) continues, "must re-envision and re-imagine themselves as cyclical corporations, whose products either literally disappear into harmless components, or whose products are so specific and targeted to a specific function that there is no spillover effect, no waste, no random molecules dancing in the cells of wildlife, in other words, no forms of life must be adversely affected."

What is true of corporations, we add, is also true of nations and states. The reader will please allow us to repeat ourselves: Texas uses more electricity than any other state; more gasoline, more coal, more natural gas than any other state; it produces more municipal waste (let's face it: *garbage*) than any other state per capita by a factor of one-third; more air toxic releases than any other state. It uses more energy than most nations on this globe: more than Great Britain, more than Italy, more than Canada. Meanwhile, Texas utilities spend a whopping 0.003 (three-tenths of one percent) of their incomes on energy efficiency programs—and complain about that! Anyone who does not think this record can be improved on has simply never thought about it.

■ ■ ■

Does Hawken's vision of the ecology of commerce sound far-fetched? Some readers might think he makes us look like hard-bitten realists. Many thanks! In fact, there is at least one industrial democracy, Germany, that is well on the way toward constructing a green economy. We will close this section with the example of Germany. When it comes to building a new tomorrow, Texans do not have to reinvent the wheel (Moore and Miller 1994).

The greening of the German economy begins, perhaps, in the early 1970s in Arizona, at the Cholla I power plant. Under the pressure of rising air quality standards, American utilities began the search for technologies that would remove pollutants from stack gases. By 1980, after several hundred millions of dollars had been invested, the processes were perfected. But utilities had been active on the political front, too. In the interim, laws had been passed which allowed utilities to build higher stacks, thus dispersing pollution over wider areas in dilute concentrations. While no long-term solution, since the pollution was not eliminated, "high-rise chimneys" were expedient. The new technologies that actually removed toxic gases and particulates from emissions were sold to the Germans.

Today, most wall board in Germany ("sheetrock," as we call it) is made from the solids precipitated out of stack gases. Here we have almost a text-book example of the principles of *Agenda 21* and the ecology of commerce at work. Through the generation of electricity and the production of wall board, jobs are being provided, profits are being made and returned to investors, air quality is maintained without the constant intrusive oversight efforts of expensive bureaucracies, thus protecting human health and pocketbooks, and natural ecosystems are protected from acid rain. And what of the American utilities (and taxpayers, who subsidized the research)? They folded a winning hand. Germany now owns the technology.

But that's only the beginning. Despite the massive expenditures required to bring East Germany's obsolete manufacturing plants up to contemporary standards, the Germans are well on their way to a real greening of the economy. Consider just a few examples. The Ford plant in Cologne uses a painting technology that saves $60 per car by keeping the paint in a closed loop (the air is recycled), thus recapturing vapors that otherwise would pollute the air. Further, under the "take back" program, a federal law that mandates recycling, German factories are now building automobiles that can be disassembled for recycling in less than twenty minutes. (Even "Hacksaw" Reynolds, a former L.A. Ram who once sawed a car in half, couldn't match that time.) But recycling covers virtually everything in the German economy, from used film canisters and cameras to plastic milk jugs and food wrap. More than 90 percent of all metals and glass and 80 percent of all paper and plastics are currently being recycled. Further, given the costs of recycling, many companies have totally redesigned their packaging, eliminating the use of cardboard containers and plastic wraps consistent with the need to protect products for health reasons.

The German government has also instituted the Blue Angel program. This program evaluates products on the basis of environmental criteria, and licenses those that are meritorious, especially those offering significant ecological advantage over standard products. To date, more than 3,500 products have been licensed. German consumers have responded favorably. Blue Angel products have in some cases come to dominate markets and in others captured a significant market share. Water-based lacquers, for example, went from 1 percent to more than 40 percent of the market. Could Texas start a Blue Armadillo program?

Beyond the Blue Angel initiative, the government is implementing carbon taxes, raising highway and bridge tolls, and offering discount fares for mass transit—a coordinated initiative designed to lower the use of private automobiles. (With its focus on mass transit, the government has not to date encouraged the development of nonexplosive fuel cells designed to hold hydrogen. In Texas, hydrogen-powered private transportation seems to offer all the environmental benefits of mass transit in a more cost-effective way.) In comparison to cars, trains reduce fuel consumption and air pollution by nearly 75 percent and require only 7.5 percent of the land required for roadways.

We do not mean to imply that Germany is heaven on earth, that German consumers have escaped the hold of conspicuous consumption, or that German business executives have slipped the hold of a bottom line mentality. But the greening of the German economy has been so successful, leading to the technological reinvigoration of manufacturing and a favorable competitive positioning of German products on the international market, that some experts describe the initiative as economic rather than environmental policy. Most important, Germany provides a concrete, real world example of the theory developed in Chapter 4: *good economics and good ecology are one and the same.* The question, more than anything, is one of the political will to make changes.

Institutionalizing Land Ethics: Practical Remedies

The remainder of this chapter examines three specific ways to institutionalize land ethics in the Lone Star State. Following the guidelines of encouraging behavior that protects the integrity, stability, and beauty of the land community, the remedies we recommend are consistent with the institutions of private property and democratic governance. One of these is as simple as "getting the price right," that is, pricing goods and services in a way that internalizes ecological costs rather than passing them on to this and future generations. Our second proposal, land-use planning, is both more complicated and politically contentious. Our third—which will sound naive in some quarters, but which we think holds great hope—is citizen initiative, including cooperation among landowners. Together they constitute ready means by which the principles of a green economy and a sustainably green earth can be realized in Texas.

Getting the Price Right. The mythology of the frontier economy is that selfish producers, guided only by *the profit motive*, and equally selfish consumers, guided only by the principle of maximizing their *individual interest*, interact in ways that lead to the best of all possible worlds. Accordingly, governmental regulation is an interference with the orderly and predictable operation of the market. Unimpeded, the market will produce the greatest good for the greatest number, guided by nothing else than the invisible hand. All hail laissez-faire theory and the invisible hand of supply and demand.

True enough, as the invisible hand metaphor suggests, the actions of individuals acting solely on the basis of selfish interests can aggregate in ways that exceed simple arithmetic sums. Much of what Adam Smith advocates in the now classic *The Wealth of Nations* has come to pass (at least at the level of textbook theory). For example, when a single manufacturer creates a product that consumers desire, that business profits enormously (since competition is limited). Those consumers who can afford the desired product, in cooperation with the producer, create a market. But markets (remember: markets are theoretically free from government interference) beget competition, and soon other producers—drawn by the lure of profits—enter, adding new productive capacity and creating new jobs. As competition increases, prices drop, encouraging more consumption, thereby producing more profits (although the profit margin diminishes) and leading to yet another round of investment and job creation. In textbook terms, this is the invisible hand at work, fostering a dynamic growth-oriented society.

The problem with the invisible hand is the "invisible foot." While textbook theory acknowledges the dynamic interrelation of individual consumers and producers in creating markets, as well as the competitive process that drives investment in productive capital, job creation, and better products for lower prices, nowhere does it recognize that the synergy of producers and consumers can also create undesired (and potentially catastrophic) effects. For example, producers might gain a price advantage over competitors by using child labor—or even slaves. Similarly, producers might offer lower-priced goods to consumers by dumping toxic byproducts into the water or discharging them into the air. Or, one firm might corner the market, drive out competition, and raise prices to suit itself.

Even a cursory knowledge of American history, regardless of how one interprets this history, shows that society came to recognize that the exploitation of children and the idea that one class of human beings could hold others in bondage were morally wrong. Child labor laws, while abominations on the face of the pure market, were the consequence: society interfered, with good reason, in the unregulated operation of the market. However controversial at the time, and whatever the disruption of the manufacturers exploiting child labor—the coal mining industry was perhaps the worst offender—the consequences have been positive over the long run.

Similarly, Americans made judgments during the 1970s that manufacturers (as well as municipalities and individuals) should cease and desist from the practice of disposing of toxics by venting them into the commons. Just as with child labor laws, clean air and water laws represent—from the laissez-faire standpoint—an unspeakable intrusion. But society's judgment was that the unregulated market was producing environmental conditions that were not only morally wrong but ecologically disastrous.

The point is simply this: American history confirms again and again that the market, whatever its many virtues, is not a sacred institution beyond criticism and correction. Public values and moral judgment have repeatedly led to policies designed to reform the practice of producers and consumers.

"Getting the price right" means that, as a minimum, we recognize that the economy and ecology are not separate but dynamically interlocked systems. We recognize that what we do as producers and consumers, in other words, affects our local and regional (as well as national and even global) ecosystems. For example, at present we are dependent on energy derived from hydrocarbons to run industrial plants and cool homes as well as for transportation; yet at some level of emission and concentration, greenhouse gases will lead to global climate change. The authors do not assume that producers and consumers are either malevolent souls or misguided Dr. Strangeloves. We believe that Texas producers and consumers take their signals from the market. Which is just the problem, since the economy and ecology are at present decoupled: they do not, in other words, dynamically interrelate in a rational way. Utilities have no incentive to invest in solar, wind, and other alternative energy technologies. Manufacturers have no incentive to reduce toxic emissions. Consumers have no incentive to purchase products that are designed according to the commerce of ecology: earth-friendly products typically carry a price premium rather than savings.

But prices could reflect ecological costs. And price changes could be implemented in relatively short order within the confines of the presently existing system.

Various costs need to be incorporated into prices: one is costs resulting from "spillover effects." For example, when a regional water authority dams a free-running river, altering not only the timing of the water flow but its contents, downstream effects on the fertility of the Gulf fishery and the integrity of coastal wetlands are a given conclusion. Consumers who eat at fast food burger emporiums also create spillovers, often in regions—such as Amazon rainforest cleared for pasture—thousands of miles distant from the local Burger King. Mothers and fathers driving their kids to school and themselves to work create spillovers. And so on in an endless cycle of ecological effects that are disconnected from market prices.

Economists claim that spillover effects are difficult to measure, a point we are willing to concede. In Chapter 4 we cited an estimate from the Union of Concerned Scientists that each gallon of gasoline used carries an uncosted component of $2.53. Critics could justifiably argue that such an estimate promotes belief in a false numerical accuracy. The point that the critics miss, however, is this: whatever the difficulty in measuring ecological costs, it is patently irrational not to attempt to price them.

The National Commission on the Environment (as we noted above, a prestigious blue ribbon panel constituted of scientists, environmental economists, and corporate CEOs) recommends that states should incrementally implement (at the rate of $0.20/year) a gasoline tax of $1 per gallon (1993). The commission concedes that precisely predicting the effects—economic, environmental, and social—of such a tax is difficult. The tax might need to be increased. Or lowered.

Clearly it would begin to promote the more conservative and efficient use of gasoline, thereby reducing the emission of carbon dioxide and other noxious gases. That alone might be an adequate payoff. But there are many other positive effects as well. For one, such a tax would eliminate the need for further tinkering with the CAFE (Corporate Average Fuel Economy) standards, standards which have been enormously difficult to enforce and which are undercut by a wide variety of exceptions. Further, vulnerability to the vagaries of, as well as the balance of trade problems created by, foreign oil imports could be reduced. And perhaps most importantly, such tax monies, if reinvested in the development of alternative energy and transportation technologies, might lead Texans and the rest of America in a sustainable direction.

Land-use Planning. In the United States, and especially in Texas, where the frontier mythology lives on, the rights of private property have been virtually absolute. Yet private property only exists within the reality of historical process: the institution, in other words, is a social creation, first imagined by human beings in particular times and places, and modified through time by successive generations.

What is land-use planning? Many things, actually: our argument focuses on ecologically oriented land-use planning, the kind of planning that would help Texas redirect economic activities that are ecologically destructive (see Caldwell and Shrader-Frechette 1993; LaFreniere 1993). But, as the twelve principles discussed above imply, economic uses of the land that destroy ecosystem integrity are short-sighted and self-defeating. So framed, land-use planning is the middle ground between reckless exploitation that destroys the resource and dogmatic preservation which locks up the land as a wilderness enclave.

Of course, society increasingly values designated wilderness areas, partly as a consequence of three centuries of relentless humanization: excluding Alaska, less than 5 percent of the American landmass is wilderness. To many Americans, our sense of national identity requires preserving at least some of the wild places that helped shape our nation's destiny. We find the idea of a nation covered with parking lots and shopping malls, clearcuts and waste dumps, to be repugnant. Leopold writes in his classic *Game Management* (1986):

> We of the industrial age boast of our control over nature. Plant or animal, star or atom, wind or river—there is no force in earth or sky which we will not shortly harness to build "the good life" for ourselves.
>
> But what is the good life? Is all this glut of power to be used for only bread-and-butter ends? Man cannot live by bread, or Fords, alone. Are we too poor in purse or spirit to apply some of it to keep the land pleasant to see, and good to live in?

We emphasize that land-use planning is not just about wilderness preservation. We believe the creation of a sustainable society necessarily involves ecological foresight that concerns itself with the dynamic interrelations between soil and plants, air and water, plants and animals, and humans—in short, a way of thinking that goes beyond either a narrowly economic or a narrowly preservationist framework.

.   .   .

What would it mean to plan for the integrity, stability, and beauty of the land community? Land-use planning involves a variety of issues, including mass transit, water resources, wilderness refuges, soil conservation, ecosystem preservation, siting of factories, urban renewal, housing codes, architectural design, and park development—so many issues that any attempt to focus on the specifics is impossible. Entire books are dedicated to each of these issues.

Yet, viewed in an ecological way, all of these separate issues constitute a single pattern. Where and how we construct our homes and site our factories and build our roads directly influences the spatial and temporal scale of energy use, pollution, species extinction, and ecosystem degradation: ecology is, in this sense, a single piece. Land use has fragmented into a thousand and one different pieces, such as housing developments that cover more and more areas surrounding metropolitan areas, highway construction that encourages further spread of low-density land use, and the proliferation of regional shopping malls that offer further encouragement to sprawl development. The growth of the Giant Slurbs epitomizes this process.

Even if we assume that no one sets out to destroy the land, the consequences of sprawl development are, as we have repeatedly stressed, seriously destructive. For one, pollution from nonpoint sources, such as toxic runoff from highways and parking lots subject to torrential rains, steadily increases. Controlling toxics from identifiable sources, such as petrochemical factories, is difficult; controlling toxics emitted from a million sources is almost impossible. Sprawl development also destroys habitat, partly by covering the land with houses, malls, and roads, and partly by fragmenting ecosystems with development that does not consider such issues as minimum viable populations, endangered species, migratory pathways, and the diminished ability of ecosystems to resist disturbance.

Such planning and zoning requirements as do exist are largely issue-specific, such as regulations governing the siting of multifamily housing, shopping centers, adult entertainment establishments, and schools. Often particular parts of the land community are protected, such as wetlands, refuges for migratory waterfowl, and scenic river corridors. But these efforts, however important, are fragmentary. More than one critic has argued that such "land-use planning" is more a blueprint for setting *the rate* of environmental ruination than actual protection.

A single issue, groundwater, perfectly illustrates the gap between misguided land-use planning and ecologically informed land-use planning. Unlike surface water controls, where at least some of the principles of ecology enter into consideration, the regulation of groundwater is in, at best, an embryonic stage. Because groundwater is buried, out of sight, the common law tradition granted absolute right of ownership: anyone owning a Texas wellhead has the legal right to unlimited pumping (with the one exception noted in Chapter 2). Which is to say that the question of water allocation from aquifers has basically been conflated with the question of water rights. Nowhere do considerations of sustainable rates of pumping enter the decision-making loop. Nowhere in Texas is the quantity of underground water even monitored. Meanwhile, the federal government continues to subsidize the extraction of groundwater by private enterprise.

Even federal statutes regulating groundwater are relatively primitive. While the Clean Water Act (1972) controls the pollution of surface waters, groundwater is not explicitly included. One consequence is that pollution laws governing groundwater are essentially a hodgepodge. William Goldfarb (1992), a leading authority on groundwater regulation, argues that the most important questions concerning land-use planning for groundwater are never asked. Among these are questions of economic costs (who pays) and benefits (who reaps profits), environmental costs (who pays) and benefits (who gains), and the implications of knowledge of hydroecological limits and the precautionary principle. Further, Goldfarb argues, land-use planning, historically dominated by economic and engineering interests, must be expanded to allow for multiple interests. And domains of expertise. He envisions multidisciplinary teams, including "persons educated in communications, ecology, economics, engineering, ethics, geology, hydrology, information systems, law, planning, politics, public administration, public health, public participation, and sociology and social psychology," as necessary for making rational decisions. Of course, such comprehensive decision-making for management of groundwater resources flies in the face of established procedures. "Groups favoring groundwater extraction and development," Goldfarb continues, favor business as usual, and "resist widening the contexts of decisions that affect their financial interests." Keep the water flowing, is their attitude, and let posterity take care of itself.

Out of the many land-use factors that cry out to be thought through and dealt with effectively in Texas, we will mention two others: coastal zone management and floodplain development. Both are "live options": something could be done about them, given the current social and economic situation in the state. Both, if not dealt with, can have very costly results.

Not many years ago one of the authors of this book served for a year on the Texas Land Commissioner's Coastal Zone Management Commission: a group of business people, scientists, and citizen environmentalists attempting to find ways of protecting the state's coastal wetlands and estuaries. Virtually untouched at the end of World War II, they have come under increasing assault from any number of quarters. Damming of rivers upstream has diminished both water flow and the "sand budget" which replenish, respectively, their bays and their barrier islands. Dredging and landfill have significantly disturbed the Coastal Zone's function as a source of shellfish and a natural hatchery for game fish. Pollution from cities and from petrochemical plants, construction projects, and massive population increase (brought to bear helter-skelter) all take their toll. As we have said above, much of this is not apparent from the highway. The proceedings of the Coastal Zone Management Commission made it painfully clear that these were not myths or fabrications. They were—and are—real problems.

If representatives of major corporations served on this commission, it was because it was in their interest to do so. Many sincerely wished to protect the Coastal Zone and its riches. The overriding concern of business, however, was what might be called a level playing field: a consistent set of expectations within which it is possible to invest without uncertainty. This involves two factors: (1) A clear public policy that guides planning. (2) A definite calendar. Planning would let business interests know what locations were out of bounds for development: industrial, residential, or other. A calendar would let business know—in borderline cases, for example—within a definite and reasonably brief time, whether a certain area could be developed or not.

Barring such definite guidelines, business is beset by damaging uncertainties. To take only the problem of the calendar: typically, business must borrow money, and at interest. If the investment cannot be recouped in a reasonably short time, interest costs will become prohibitive, derailing projects, sometimes even leading to bankruptcy. If the governmental agencies in charge of protecting the environment cannot agree, if bureaucratic red tape or court battles delay a definite decision indefinitely, the result can be disaster for those who invest the money. Not exactly an endearing prospect.

If business has an obligation to protect the environment, environmentalists have an obligation to provide business with clear regulations and prompt enforcement.

As it happened, the effort to create a Texas Coastal Zone management plan failed. Conservationists and scientists were grudgingly willing to go along with a plan which seemed to them not tough enough; business interests recoiled, fearing destructive regulation. The state was the loser. The Texas General Land Office was directed by the legislature in 1991 to develop a Coastal Zone Management Plan, expected to come into effect in the fall of 1996. Regulation of the Coastal Zone is still by a patchwork of local, state, and federal agencies and laws. Such can scarcely protect the integrity or stability of the region. Or its beauty. All three are necessary to a region which annually sustains a two billion dollar tourist trade and a two to three hundred million dollar fishery.

If land-use management could make possible the sustainable use of the Coastal Zone, it would do wonders for the Lone Star State's floodplains. We will discuss this subject at greater length in dealing with the Big Thicket of Southeast Texas. Here we will be brief and to the point. Minnesota is literally a land of lakes. It has rivers—including a Red River—to be sure. But its rocky glaciated terrain is ideal for ponds, lakes, and marshes, many connected. Texas, by contrast, is almost devoid of natural lakes. It is a land of rivers.

It is said that when Will Rogers first saw the Trinity River, at Dallas, his response was, "Pave it." His quip is proof positive that he saw the Trinity in the dry summer months, when paving the trickle of water seems an easy task. In the spring, the idea of paving it is almost funny. Then the Trinity becomes a powerful giant: breaking levees, inundating bottomlands, invading subdivisions.

And so it is with almost all our creeks and rivers. Living in either feast or famine, they are either shallow and peaceful or wild and wide. Early explorers and later merchants, who tried to use them as highways, discovered this to their despair. A stream that could be navigated in April or May might be impossible to travel in September and October. It might even have ceased to exist.

The point of this for land-use planning is that Texas bottomlands do not lend themselves to development. In some cases they make a dubious investment for agriculture. Everything that one puts into the land, or onto it, is liable to end up downstream: in the worst case, in the Gulf of Mexico. This makes some floodplains suitable largely for paying taxes on. It makes virtually all floodplains unsuitable for development. It also suggests that the best course, in many cases, is to leave floodplains in Texas as greenbelts, or even as wilderness.

The existence of Federal Floodplain Insurance, which leads people to build in low areas and then obligates the government to repair or rebuild their residences or vacation homes, is a further reason to make flood-prone areas into greenbelts. Otherwise the body politic is obligated to pay lowland residents over and over to repair or rebuild. Not only hikers, canoers, birdwatchers, or fishers should consider land-use planning in this case. Fiscal conservatives should too.

Which brings us full circle, to where the state of neglect, the principles that underlie the ecology of commerce, and ecologically oriented land-use planning meet. As we envision it, land-use planning that facilitates the institutionalization of land ethics does not mean that all the land is locked up in perpetuity, although Americans and Texans clearly have interests in some designated wilderness areas. Rather, it means that we begin to use the land in ways, as Leopold envisioned, that do not spoil it, so that it is good to live in, and so that nature's economy and the human economy are complementary rather than antagonistic.

Some proponents of ecological land-use planning argue for the "principle of thirds": one-third of the land should be designated wilderness, one-third should be habitat used for purposes of agriculture, and one-third allocated for intense human settlement. On this model, core areas of wilderness function to sustain biodiversity and speciation itself, that is, the ongoing evolutionary process that produces new life forms. Humanized landscapes (agriculture, forestry, reservoirs) yield economic benefits, but they also serve as buffer zones between wilderness areas and the densely populated areas of human settlement. This model has pluses; for example, it serves as a focus for political debate and helps to focus scientific research. But the model also has negatives; for example, it seems too abstract, even mechanical, to guide actual land-use planning, particularly since the world in which we live is already in use.

The goal of ecologically oriented land-use planning is to redirect land use in ways that bar selfish interests from short-term exploitation that destroys the land's long-term economic utility and ecological integrity. As the ecology of commerce implies, nature was a self-sustaining biophysical enterprise long before human beings existed. The fatal flaw of the present economic paradigm is that it is unequivocally destroying the self-sustaining processes that are the dynamic heart of ecosystem integrity. Land-use planning thus aims at preserving the integrity and stability of the land community. This goal, we must emphasize, is not inconsistent with human welfare, but in fact is essential to sustaining human welfare over the long term.

Citizen Initiative. Not all environmental goals require laws and governments for their realization. Many are within the reach of individuals: large or small landowners, teachers, land managers, game managers, ranchers, farmers, developers. The possibilities here are legion, and, we are convinced, have only just begun to be utilized. The fact that we mention them last does not mean that we think they are of least importance.

A few examples will help. We know a biology teacher at a rural community college who encourages his students, for credit, to build up a county herbarium, that is, a list, with specimens, of every plant growing in that county: where it grows, when it flowers, how many there are. The end result will not only be to increase significantly their knowledge of the plants in that county (including any that are rare, scarce, or endangered, or existing beyond their ordinary "range"); it will be to produce Texans with a vivid sense of, and pride in, the plants of their state. To these, the reflections of a Leopold can be not merely abstract or figurative, but concrete, and real. What this teacher has done for one county, however, could be done for many—in fact, for all 254 in the state. There would then be not only a factual basis for the conservation of plant species in the state, but more citizens prepared to understand why such conservation is wise.

We know another person—a lady in North Texas—whose sympathies lead in a similar direction. A house which she owned, adjacent to the one she lived in, was in very sad condition; as she put it, the termites were holding hands just to keep it from falling down. Rather than build a new house in place of the old, she had the old house torn down and turned the lot into a bird sanctuary, with sufficient water and native plants to support a thriving population of many avian species. Both her neighborhood and the birds are the beneficiaries of her act. Only the local insect populations seem to suffer.

We know a third individual—a rancher along the Red River—who is considering turning his land into a nature sanctuary. He would not be the first to have done so in Texas. The Welder Wildlife Refuge near Sinton and the Heard Nature Sanctuary near McKinney are well-known examples. But his land not only borders the Red River; it contains parts of two creeks that empty into the river. One would thus have not only an extremely rich and diverse area for nature studies and nature teaching: one would also have the beginnings of a possible "greenbelt" along the river, one which could prevent "development," fragmentation, and general degrading of that environment.

There is a very sound response to even the idea of such a possibility: namely, that it is unwise to "lock up" such valuable farm and grazing land in perpetuity, that to do so would be to undermine the local economy. We agree. But it is not necessary, in protecting stream corridors, to lock up an entire countryside. Nor is there any need to displace local families. Scenic easements and/or conservation easements can protect wooded creeksides and riverbottom forests while leaving adjacent lands open for grazing or farming. Such a pattern, available to landowners in many parts of the Lone Star State, could protect stream corridors in perpetuity. It can involve the donation of land; or it can involve, simply, legal agreements to manage certain areas "environmentally." We add, that where individuals manage land wisely, there can be no argument for bringing in government to manage things better.

The three cases cited here—of a biologist, a suburban landowner, a rancher—barely scratch the surface. We know of an elementary school in Round Rock whose students and teachers are trying to preserve 20 acres of blackland prairie. We know of garden clubs and hunting clubs that have made special efforts to defend—often by purchase—valuable forest habitat. Though it is true that many factors, economic and legal and political, have to be taken into account in making a land ethic real, we would like to think that the efforts and concerns of many individuals can make a profound—perhaps the profoundest—difference.

Conclusion

The burden of proof that land ethics are impractical lies on those who are psychologically wedded to the past. We have advanced and defended the notion that land ethics are not only practical but that ready means exist to begin their institutionalization. The first step in building a sustainable Texas does not require draconian, totalitarian solutions, but simply the resolution by Texans to institutionalize land ethics in the market itself by getting the price right. As we argued, greening the economy does not hinder commerce but actually restructures commerce in a way that is ecologically feasible: good ecology is good business. Ecologically oriented land-use planning that escapes the hold of fragmentary, piecemeal thinking is essential, too. Getting the price right helps to move producers and consumers in the right direction, but the market cannot alone achieve the ends of integrity, stability, and beauty.

We believe that time is of the essence. Citizens, if they are committed to place and empowered by the land ethic, can build a new Texas that throws off the frontier mythology or, if unwilling to rethink their prior assumptions, can face environmental consequences of an increasingly severe and costly nature. Chapter 7 briefly looks at the possibilities for tomorrow.

Clearcut on Cotton Road at boundary of 26,000-acre Lance Rosier Unit, Big Thicket.

6

THE BIG THICKET

Having suggested that ecology and economics can learn to march along together, we thought it would be a good idea to provide an example of a situation in which ecology and economics might, at least conceivably, come to a mutual understanding. This case is the Big Thicket region of Southeast Texas, where a number of forces have come together to suggest an ecologically sustainable future. Besides: not only is the Big Thicket a colorful and exciting place; Aldo Leopold (we have discovered) explored it in its original purity, before it was mined by lumber interests and scarred by oil operations. He liked it. So do we.

East Texas (the Woodlands) does not seem to fit the state's image. Texas is, or is supposed to be, West. East Texas is South. Texas is supposed to be dry, and rocky: a place of scrub oak and mesquite, mesa and chaparral. East Texas is moist, and alluvial, and rich with forest.

Texas is a place of broad views, seeking distant horizons. In East Texas the land and the forest make for closure, limitation, close acquaintance. Texas projects an image of frontier, of motion, of conquest. In East Texas a faint mist hangs in the air, pine scent drifts with the wind. A strange timelessness pervades the senses.

But if East Texas does not fit the state's image, the part of it we are going to describe in this chapter—Southeast Texas, the Big Thicket—seems entirely inconsistent with anything that could conceivably be called the Lone Star State. Yet it exists, like a part of William Faulkner's wild Mississippi Delta, a piece of the Deep South set down on the edge of the post oak country and the Western prairies.

Some History, Including Environmental History

The lush, dense country was noticeably different from the beginning. The Indians called it the Big Woods. Spanish padres at Nacogdoches described it as a forest between their missions at Nacogdoches and the Gulf so thick that Indians hunting there went only by canoe and did not remain long. There may be some truth in the padres' reports. Archaeological surveys have so far found little evidence of permanent settlement in the "Thicket" prior to the coming of Europeans. The region seems to have been a no-man's land between the Caddoes to the north and the Karankawas, Patiri, and Deadose to the south. Traversed by all, it seems to have been claimed by none.

To the southeast of the Big Thicket lay a disputed area called the Neutral Ground. Bounded by the Arroyo Hondo to the east, the Gulf of Mexico to the south, and the Sabine River to the west, it was a "leftover" from the Louisiana Purchase, owned neither by the United States nor Spain and—in theory—administered by both. In fact, it was administered by bandits. So lawless was the Neutral Ground that in 1810 and 1811 military expeditions had to be staged to control it. Driven from the Neutral Ground, the drifters, outlaws, and adventurers who had taken refuge there fled to the Big Thicket and nearby areas. The "Thicket" not surprisingly took on some of the Neutral Ground's dark reputation.

The fate of the Neutral Ground's refugees was to be that of many others, who came later. The Big Thicket was to function as a wilderness redoubt, for all those who for whatever reason sought to escape the entanglements of civilization. Indians made their last stand there, clinging to the end to their nomadic independence. (The last were finally forced into a reservation in 1903.) Escaped slaves, outlaws, backwoodsmen despising the effete, imprisoning towns, trappers, professional hunters, all found free latitude behind the green walls of forest, swampland, and winding bayou. As late as the 1950s escapees from the state penitentiary at Huntsville headed for the Thicket, steps ahead of the baying hounds. As late as the First and Second World Wars, sons of local settlers sat out the conflict in remote swamps and river bends, protected and supplied by their families. They were only doing what many of their ancestors had done before them during the Civil War: hiding out, waiting, becoming scarce.

Such a sanctuary could not last forever. The assault was begun in the decade before the Civil War, as bottomland trees were felled and floated downstream during high water to sawmills nearer the Gulf. Full-scale timbering had to wait several decades, however. The East Texas Railroad was torn up for scrap during the Civil War. Railroads did not arrive again until the 1880s.

When they did, timbering began on an unheard-of scale. Near the main rail lines—or within reach of them—sawmills were built; from the sawmills "trunk lines" were laid down, fanning out radially into the forests, following the cutting of the trees. When the forests that could be reached from the railroad trunk lines were exhausted, the tracks were taken up and the lumber mill dismantled, and moved on to remaining unmined forest. In the words of biologist Claude A. McLeod (1967):

> [B]y the beginning of the 1900s, the Big Thicket loblolly pine hardwood forest, the adjacent shortleaf pine–hardwood forest to the west and north, and the magnificent longleaf pine forest contiguous on the northeast and east were under sustained assault that was not to end until practically all of the virgin pine forests were reduced to cutover woodlands.

Cutover is the operative word. No grown trees were left, not even along area streams. Only the most remote and possibly unsaleable isolated patches of forest remained. Nor was there replanting. As so often happened with Texas natural resources, the forests were "mined"; what remained were forests of stumps.

Luckily for the environmental integrity of the region, all this could not be completed at once. If some areas were leveled in the 1840s, others were not scalped until the 1880s or 1930s or even '40s. Many areas—aided by the region's 50-inch-plus rainfall, sandy loams, and nearly tropical climate—were able to regrow into something approaching their original richness. Meantime—starting in 1900 at the famous Spindletop field south of Beaumont and spreading northwestward into the Thicket at Sour Lake (1900), Saratoga (1903), and Batson (1904)—a second force entered the region: oil, with its shanty settlements, pipelines, and oil and salt overflows. In a sense, oil and timbering were two versions of the same thing: an "extractive" economy, quick to appropriate raw materials and oblivious to the results. Oil drilling, however, operated differently and had different results. Lumber operations and lumber towns were orderly and efficient. Oil, by stark contrast, transformed once isolated crossroads into roaring boomtowns, knee deep in mud, drilling rigs, tent saloons, and mule teams straining in harness. The effects of lumbering gradually faded, as new forests grew. The effects of oil fade only slowly, if at all. Many are still marked clearly on the land: barren acreage underlain by saltwater and oil sediment, where the earth is still raw clay or sand, or where trees and bushes grow only until their roots reach the black, viscous mud underground, and then die. It is a strange sight to see old oil fields and oil field overflow ponds surrounded by a tangle of trees and brush, some dead, some green and awaiting their demise.

The oil boom disappeared even more quickly than the lumber railroads and the lumber mills. Small towns lapsed back into obscurity as oil field workers left. Trains ran less often. Second-growth lumber regrew. The Big Thicket fell off into a sleep that lasted forty years.

All this was done with scarcely a voice raised in protest. When environmentalism came to the Thicket it came late. There were to be two environmental movements specifically focused there, the first beginning in 1927 and then fading, the second beginning in 1964 and continuing. But before providing an overview of conservationism and its opposite, it would make sense to explain what the long-term struggle was about. Just what is the Big Thicket, beyond being a sanctuary? Can it lay claim to special value?

Definition of a Place

Many locales in the United States possess a wide diversity of plants and animals; many are "ecotones": that is, regions of transition between contrasting terrains and climates. Of these, the Big Thicket is undoubtedly the most diverse and, if one can stretch the meaning of a term, the most transitional. A 1967 National Park Service study states:

> The forest contains elements common to the Florida Everglades, the Okefenoke Swamp, the Appalachian region, the Piedmont forests, and the large open woodlands of the coastal plains. Some large areas resemble tropical jungles in the Mexican states of Tamaulipas and Vera Cruz.

A more thorough survey would have added intrusions of different sorts of natural prairies, and of a unique "arid sandland" replete with yucca, cacti, bluejack oak, and a dozen varieties of West Texas wildflowers.

Another way of assessing the diversity of a region is not only through the similarity of its parts with whole regions elsewhere, but via the sheer complexity of its structure. Professors Thomas Eisner and Paul Feeny argued in a 1972 congressional hearing:

> It is fair to say that though the region lacks spectacular natural grandeur it is from an ecological standpoint better deserving of preservation than any exist-

ing National Park in the United States, with the possible exception of the Florida Everglades. Nowhere else is there found such of diversity of plant and animal species: nowhere else is there such a unique combination of habitats, northern temperate and subtropical and western and humid southeastern, freshwater and saltwater, forest and prairie, calcareous and acid.

Preservation of rare, scarce, and endangered species might justify the setting aside of large tracts of the Big Thicket. But the area's "incomparable ecological diversity" provides the basic argument for its protection. It is this factor, above all, which led the United Nations in 1981 to declare it an international Man and the Biosphere Reserve.

But diversity is not the only rationale. There is also sheer richness and abundance. These are stressed by Donovan S. Correll, speaking at a congressional hearing in Beaumont (1970):

> Only a few miles to the west of here as we hit the prairies, not too far. This is the utmost western limit of a great many species which are indigenous from Maryland to Florida to east Texas, and for some unknown reason which no one has really worked up yet, there is a great burst of jungle-like environment here, in fact, it is an optimum development of this vast area, in which the Government does not own, so far as I know, any essential area as a park.

In the Thicket one has, then, not only diversity, but the massive flourishing of diversity. Life there tends toward the lush, the massive, the abundant. Tends, if brush hogs and power saws can be kept out long enough for nature to regrow.

But there is still another way to define and defend an area's character: through catalogues of its denizens. We will try to keep the list short but will at least spell out the major details. The Big Thicket region contains: 110 species of overstory (tall, dominant) trees; 200 species of shrubs and understory (shorter, dependent) trees; 300 bird species (many migratory); over 30 species of ferns, and at least as many of orchids; and 4 out of North America's 5 species of insectivorous plants. Botanists estimate that the area contains at least 1,000 species of flowering plants—a really astonishing figure, which, moreover, is not an overestimation. Before a fire destroyed its contents, an arboretum at Lamar University in Beaumont contained over 800 flowering plant species collected in the Big Thicket by Geraldine Watson and others. There was no indication that the collecting was coming to an end.

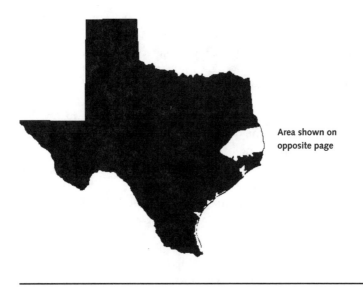

Area shown on
opposite page

Opposite: **Transposition of three maps of the Big Thicket: Biological Survey, McLeod's Ecological Analysis, and the Traditional Thicket.** From *The Big Thicket: A Challenge for Conservation,* by Pete Gunter (Austin: Jenkins Publishing Company, 1971).

Enter Clearcutting

The scars of the oil booms are fading—if slowly—from an ill-used land. The lumber barons have gone on to that great planing mill in the sky. What, then, is to prevent the "Thicket" from growing back into its original luxuriance, or at least from maintaining its original biological identity? There are of course many factors: highways, dams, massive new lake acreage, urban sprawl, forest clearing for agriculture. But the greatest of these is clearcutting. The emergence of clearcutting marks a new epoch in the environmental history of the region. It signals the start of a frantic race between environmentalists and lumber companies or, more profoundly, between public education and a new, potentially destructive technology.

If older "cut and get out" methods left forests of stumps in their wake, they had at least one benign result: the original forest type could, and as we pointed out above, usually did, regrow. With clearcutting this is no longer possible. The diverse original forests, with their understories of small trees and shrubs and their rich growth of vines, flowers, and ferns, are removed once and for all by clearcutting. The end result is a monoculture: one tree species, usually pine.

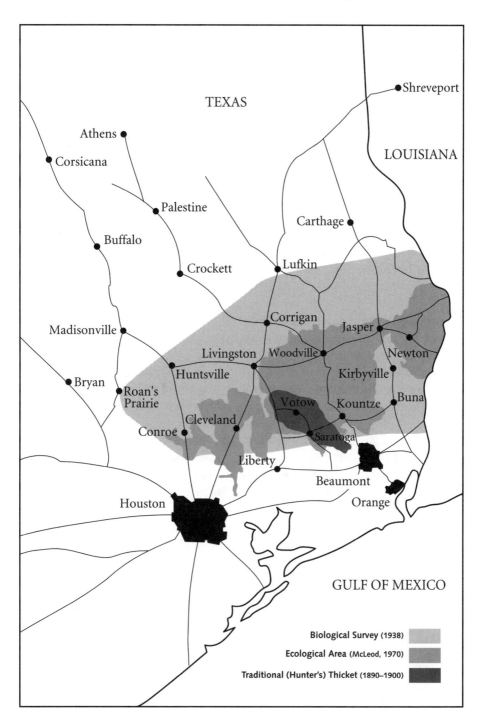

TEXAS

● Shreveport

LOUISIANA

Athens ●

● Corsicana

● Palestine

Carthage ●

Buffalo ●

● Crockett

Lufkin ●

● Corrigan

Jasper

Madisonville ●

Livingston ● Woodville ● Newton

● Bryan

Huntsville Kirbyville

Roan's Prairie

Votow ● Kountze ● ● Buna

Cleveland ●

Conroe ● Saratoga ●

Liberty ●

Beaumont

Houston

Orange

GULF OF MEXICO

Biological Survey (1938)

Ecological Area (McLeod, 1970)

Traditional (Hunter's) Thicket (1890–1900)

Instructions on how to clearcut are easy to give. First, cut all the saleable tree species in an area. Fifty acres will do; but the authors have seen clearcuts of over 10,000 acres, so size is no issue. The timber market fluctuates and some tree species may not be saleable at the time. Bulldoze these, and all brush, greenery, and small trees, into long heaps called "windrows." Burn these windrows. This will release all sorts of pollutants into the atmosphere, including a mass of "suspended particulates" (smoke particles).

Once the land is denuded, start planting pine trees, one after the other, like rows of corn stalks. (By the way, when it comes to clearing the land of all vegetation, do not hesitate to clear off creek banks and river banks. In many cases the simplest thing to do is to just push the vegetation (dirt, roots, and all) into the waterway. If the old vegetation tries to regrow, put herbicides on it. You might do this with "guns" that inject herbicide below the bark, but this is time-consuming and expensive. The easiest way is to spray herbicides from an airplane. Herbicides are not the only chemicals useful in maintaining clearcut pine monoculture. If the southern pine bark beetle should infest your tree farm, copious doses of insecticides may be administered, although they do not seem to kill the beetles.

Clearcuts may be harvested in cycles of fifteen, twenty, or twenty-five years. Once upon a time this involved a lot of working people. Now, however, machines bite off pines at land level, toss them into a waiting truckbed, and go on. A couple of workers can do it.

Clearcutting began in East Texas in the late 1930s. But it did not begin on a massive scale there until the 1960s. That is exactly when the second Big Thicket Association was formed: in a church in Saratoga, Texas, November 13, 1964. The first such organization, the East Texas Big Thicket Association, had been formed in 1927 as a response to cut-and-get-out timbering and by the 1940s had been able to gain backing for a 430,000-acre Big Thicket National Park. But by then the Second World War had come, and a combination of war and state and federal politics killed the Big Thicket National Park movement. By the 1950s the East Texas Big Thicket Association had died a sad and quiet death. The new Big Thicket Association faced an uphill battle against an accelerating timber technology which threatened not only to destroy resplendent examples of regrown wilderness but to obliterate whole ecosystems.

Aldo Leopold in the Big Thicket

In early March 1909 Aldo Leopold and a handful of other recent graduates of the Yale Forest School arrived at a lumber camp 8 miles southwest of Doucette, Texas. They had come around Key West by boat, had spent a pleasant day in New Orleans and another socializing with the leadership and society of Beaumont. Now green palisades of the forest closed around them. Leopold and his friend P. J. Paxton ("Paxie") labored for two rainy days with just-milled lumber to build a floor, set up their tent, and build beds and other furniture. They were soon, as Leopold wrote, "a pretty sore and tired lot." Then work began, and they "got a little bit more so." It was to be no vacation. The third day was taken up with surveying and the day after with following old Spanish land lines. Those Spanish boundaries, though surveyed back in the 1830s, were still dimly visible in 1909, and the young Leopold took a great deal of pride in being able to find and follow them.

The timber in the area, Leopold wrote, was magnificent, even if they sometimes had to wade knee to waist deep through a swamp to reach it. On the eighteenth of March Leopold set out on a two-day "traverse": "We made about ten miles to the southward and got back late this evening. We had to work like the devil but had a mighty good time. We ran into a lot of hardwood and Loblolly Pine Country, with thick brush, mostly holly" (Collection: Series 9/25/10, Leopold letter of 3/18/09). The dense understory made it hard to see even short distances. The crew was, however, able to get one 2,200-foot surveyor's shot. It proved a record.

Learning to be a lumberman turned out to be complex. Surveying is not usually exhausting work. But when the terrain is jungle-like, exhaustion is inevitable. Leopold wrote (concerning a swamp community termed a "baygall"): "But when it comes to running a line across a Bay-Gall, an airship would really be preferable. They are absolutely the thickest places I have seen, and are chuck full of Wood-Ticks and Sand Flies and all other varmints" (4/3/09). But besides surveying, there were tree measurements (from which volume tables had to be prepared). This involved two-man teams, who were expected to get precise figures on twenty-five trees a day, but who often managed to account for thirty or forty. Work then shifted from the woods to the lumber mill, whose operations the young foresters were required to master.

The country Leopold and his friends traversed with so much difficulty was in the Upper (as opposed, to no one's surprise, to the Lower) Big Thicket. Their traverse would have taken them south to, or almost to, Village Creek, now scheduled to become part of the Big Thicket National Preserve. Just west and north of them was the Alabama and Coushatta Indian Reservation, a landmark Leopold seems not to have been aware of, or at least never to have mentioned. The young foresters managed to find shelter at night with a farmer named Tolar. His farm, Leopold wrote, was the most prosperous in the area: "It was mighty interesting, with the numerous hounds, the immaculate cabin under the giant magnolias, the open hearth and dutch oven cooking, the pine knot fire, the feather-beds, etc. I wish I had time to tell you all about it" (3/19/09).

If he did not have time it was because the young men got up the next morning at five o'clock and worked steadily until six o'clock that evening. After which they did reports on the day's work. There would not be time most days to write letters, except on Sundays. That was understandable. The Yale aristocrats were working twelve- to fourteen- to sixteen-hour days.

On April 27 Leopold wrote—evidently with some relief—that he now, at least, had an idea of how much there really is to know about a sawmill:

> Last Saturday Paxie and I were assigned to studying the mill machinery. Monday we were on grading. Tuesday we had to run out a survey of the yards and plant. Yesterday (Wednesday) we studied the dry kilns and dry sheds and system of yarding. Today we again were put on grading, this time working on the dressed lumber from the Planner instead of at the Sorting Table at the mill.

Grading was as much a test of mental stamina as of experience. It involved sorting out the first-quality planks from the second, third, and worst. Planks moved past while the graders hefted and turned and eyeballed them, making quick judgments. Leopold and Paxton finally achieved 75 percent accuracy and concluded, first of all, that yellow pine is very heavy wood, and second, that they could certainly learn to be graders quickly—in a month or two.

In spite of the demands of work, Leopold managed to explore the countryside. He filled his letters not only with details of lumbering lore but with descriptions of the flora and fauna he had seen. He lamented that he could not yet take up his old habit of learning new bird and plant species.

Though Leopold had representative encounters with his new environment, the isolation of the lumber camp, the close confinement with his own class of Yale forestry students, and the channeling of work through the mill limited his access to the folklore of the region. The bear hunts still going on in the Lower Big Thicket, the Indian reservation often only a long walk away, and the stories of outlaws and Confederate deserters, ghost roads and river pirates, mountain lions and giant alligators, are nowhere hinted at in his letters. His was the lore of the forest products industry.

This might, in a way, have been a blessing. We have mentioned that the exact location of the Big Thicket had shifted in the public mind from time to time. And we have used the terms "Upper" and "Lower" Big Thicket. It is time—before letting Leopold describe his acquaintance with nature in the area—to clarify these terms.

One of the big problems conservationists have had—and which Leopold would have had if he had had occasion to puzzle over it—is that of stripping away the folklore concerning the Big Thicket and defining it. Were the "Thicket" a topographic feature—a mountain, a mesa, a canyon—there would be no problem. But it is a plant growth region dependent on climate, soils, and drainage, and this requires a different sort of definition.

McLeod's definition, as worked out in his *The Big Thicket of East Texas* (1967) and later extended to include distinctive areas near the Sabine River (1970), is straightforward. The Big Thicket is, he states, a loblolly pine–hardwood association. The hardwoods he mentions are southern magnolia, beech, white oak, and in some areas swamp chestnut oak. The loblolly pine, as its name suggests, is a pine tree which grows in low, wet places. In the "Upper" Big Thicket, beech occurs with magnolias and pines; in the "Lower" Big Thicket magnolias and loblolly pine are found in conjunction with swamp chestnut oak. McLeod is able to map the confines of this forest with considerable precision. It stretches from just southwest of Conroe in Montgomery County to the north-central part of Jasper County, and from there, via various stream corridors, to the Sabine River border with Louisiana: approximately 100 miles east-west, and at its widest 40 miles north-south.

All of Leopold's adventures were in the Upper Big Thicket, which in spite of its ample swamps, seeps, creeks, and baygalls is higher, hillier, and better drained than the Lower Big Thicket. Even the transfer of his group to the Fowler farm, 5 miles east of Colmesneil (roughly, 13 miles northeast of Doucette or 21 miles from their original camp), only placed Leopold just south of the region's northern perimeter, as mapped by McLeod. Leopold (Collection: Series 9/25/10, Leopold letter of 5/23/09) gives an enthusiastic account of his experience in the higher, hillier country east of Colmesneil:

> The country up here on the north tract has got [the country around the original camp] beat a mile. There are considerable hills, with wide valleys that you can *see* across. And everywhere there is water—swift little brooks with clear cool water and clean sandy bottom—as that there is no need for going thirsty all day. The timber is big, with lots of beautiful hardwoods along the streams. Everything is very wild, and there is really considerable game. We saw lots of quail every day, a few squirrels (black, fox, and gray) and a few tracks of turkeys and deer. Snakes were very plentiful. We killed half a dozen cotton-mouths every day. . . . Black snakes and bull snakes were too thick to notice, although

one day we got one of the "Blue Racer" kind up a tree, and were trying to climb him out, when I got one of the falling clubs on the head and had good occasion to "notice" the snake.

Though the group saw some king snakes and killed a copperhead, the day's crowning achievement was the killing of a big rattlesnake, nearly 4 feet long. Leopold notes that Paxie removed its skin and placed it on the clothesline rack, where it rattled merrily in the wind.

If he found work in the swampier, thicker country south and west of Doucette harder, Leopold managed to remain cheerful. The towns he found quaint. Woodville (just south of Doucette) he describes as "a funny little town. I never saw so many dogs. Counted nine at one Street Consultation this evening. Also some Prize-Taking Razorbacks. It is a nice little place though" (4/14/09).

His grudge against razorback hogs came from the fact that they infected the lumber camp with fleas. Leopold even asked his mother to sew a sort of "sleeping sack"—one that could be buttoned up at the top—to protect him from fleabites. She dutifully sewed the sack and shipped it from Iowa.

He and his friends were more indebted to his mother for her occasional shipments of food than for her sewing. Cookies, gingerbread, canned goods disappeared the moment they reached camp. It takes courage, and accumulated resistance, they found, to withstand Southern cooking. Concerning their first meal at the Fowler farm, he writes: "the cornbread, though heavy as lead, is really eatable. Everything else is almost out of the question" (5/16/09). He notes, concerning a weekend at the camp east of Doucette, how good it was going to get a rest, and "last but not least, to eat a meal part of which at least was not *fried*. In Woodville everything is fried except the biscuits. They are just slightly singed on the outside" (4/25/09). At least he couldn't complain about being overcharged. The Stewart Hotel asked one dollar per day for three meals and a room.

In early June Leopold took his leave of Southeast Texas, never to return. If he was to write about or discuss the region again, we do not know about it. His letters home from the camp near Doucette, however, reveal a fascinating duality: an unrealized contradiction. Clearly, Leopold loves nature: loves its moods, its creatures, its harshness along with its beauty. Yet he seems at this stage in his life to see no conflict between loving it and cutting it down. The huge cypresses in Big Cypress swamp may be awesome; but he is engaged in surveys whose clear goal is to behead the entire area.

At the foot of the Yale Forest Camp was a pond that faded back insensibly into a swamp. The foresters could swim there and cool off. Leopold also found it a source of inspiration, noting the appearance there of roseate spoonbills, snowy egrets (then hunted nearly to extinction and very rare), anhingas (water turkeys), coots, gallinules, bitterns, blue herons.

> This morning I spent exploring the swamp at the head of the pond. It was hot, cloudy, muggy, and full of flies and mosquitos, yet I had a most tremendously interesting time. This pond is reputed to be an older beaver pond. I never believed it until this morning, when I found an old beaver-dam at the head of it, so old and large that it was totally grown over and almost obscured by trees and bushes. Moreover I found cuttings of young gum-trees less than two months old. There are undoubtedly a few beaver left. I am thinking of building me a boat and carefully exploring the whole proposition. (4/22/09)

Leopold never got around to building the boat, so we will never know how large the swamp was or what it contained. In his last days in camp a series of heavy rains turned the pond "too brown and smelly for swimming" (5/29/09). Bark, tannic acid, and decaying vegetation had been lifted out of the swamp and sluiced into the once clear pond.

The other area Leopold chose to explore—or rather, was required to assess for timber and to survey—was the swamp country along Big Cypress Creek:

> I have had quite an amusing day. Was sent on topographic work way down on Big Cypress Creek. It is six miles down to there. I ran lines through the Big Cypress Swamp all day, and had a very interesting time with the mud, the flies, an ungodly brand of catbrier, and a cotton-mouth moccasin, who by the way got under a log and escaped. Also saw a pileated woodpecker, and had a conversation with a great horned owl. Also saw my first black squirrel. (4/10/09)

On one trek across the swamp Leopold and his friends measured a giant cypress 17 feet 9 inches in girth (4/25/09). That is close to "champion" size. The area along Big Cypress Creek was scheduled for inclusion in a Big Thicket National Park in the early 1970s. Unfortunately it was clearcut before it could be included. One will find no huge old cypress trees there now.

The dense brush, the swamps, the hard work schedule scarcely made Leopold's stay in the "Thicket" an idyll. His gritty, realistic descriptions make this clear. Still, he found himself impressed: "It is really a beautiful region. If you could see the full moon tonight, sailing high over towering pine trees, you would like it too. I have decided, again and again, that it is worth all the trouble of the mosquitos and fleas and snakes and pigs, and more too" (5/4/09). We could only wish that he had found time to explore it further. Especially it is unfortunate, as we noted above, that he never got to sit around a campfire with local people and hear their tales.

It is symbolic that during the young forest graduates' stay at the lumber camp both Professor Graves of the Yale School of Forestry and Gifford Pinchot himself visited the camp. The occasion was a meeting of the Conservation Committee of the Southern Pine Manufacturers Association. Leopold was given the task of making sure each visiting dignitary was assigned to a particular tent and his needs taken care of. He sent his mother a list of the visitors, the forestry students, and the tents, but made no mention of their speeches or what was said: proof enough of his unquestioned assumption of Pinchot's brand of Resource Conservation Ecology.

It is not surprising. Leopold and his contemporaries, though the date was 1909 and the American land frontier had been officially closed for nearly twenty years, were still nineteenth-century Americans. It seemed both obvious and inevitable that one could be both a nature romantic and a cutter of forests, an avid hunter and a lover of wild game, a devotee of swamps and a hewer of the last big cypress trees. There seemed to be so much of it. It was hard to believe that it could ever end.

It was a blithe, simple faith that the young men took with them to the Western forests. It could only come to an end when the incredible abundance—of game, and woods, and clear, clean water—had been finally exhausted, and the results of heedless and thoughtless taking made apparent. To most people, as Leopold was clearly to recognize, a land ethic will only make sense when the end of the road looms in view.

Conservation by Intention and Conservation by Chance: Some Concluding Reflections

In a recent article (1994) in *Texas Books in Review*, former congressman Bob Eckhardt—who had both observed and participated in the Big Thicket conservation movement which restarted in 1964—sums up the frustrations of this movement succinctly. Pointing to the dark history of the Neutral Ground, he concludes that there was as much misdirection in the woods in the early Neutral Ground as there was to be in Congress, later, when the Big Thicket became a political issue: "In my 22 years as a member of legislative bodies, never can I recall an issue on which there were so many starts and stops, wins and losses as there were in this process." The authors will spare the reader a blow-by-blow account of this process. Rather, they would like to survey its results: both its potentially sad and barren results and what has actually happened and is happening. The latter—rare in environmental affairs—actually sheds a gleam of hope. There is some reason—muted but still real—for cautious optimism. We will try to explain why.

A federally sponsored survey of the region in 1936 and 1938 concluded that the original Big Thicket consisted of 3,500,000 acres sprawling westward from the Louisiana border almost to the Brazos River in Grimes County. That is no small potatoes: an area the size of Connecticut, half the size of Maryland. More recent estimates by McLeod suggest 1,800,000 or 1,850,000 acres. By the mid-1960s conservationists held that the once vast expanse was reduced to 350,000 acres and was disappearing at a rate of at least 100 acres a day. The major culprit, they claimed, was clearcutting.

If some of the cries of conservationists seemed excessively loud and piteous, and if some of their claims appeared inflated, it was still clear to most observers that the Big Thicket, whatever its original size, was now being picked apart without a thought as to its biological integrity. The remotest places now faced the power saw and the brush hog. Clearcuts with their piles of burning brush stretched in many places from horizon to horizon. Even bottomlands and creekbeds were not immune. Swamps, where possible, were being drained; beavers were being extirpated and their dams broken. To no one's great surprise, game—and many other—populations were visibly declining.

If the present was dispiriting, the future was bleak. As things then stood, it appeared that virtually all of Southeast Texas, from Interstate 45 to the Trinity River, to the Neches River, all the way to the Sabine River, was going to be clearcut. The original forests would in two or three decades simply be gone, replaced by rows of slash or loblolly pine: a transformation almost too massive to be believed, and of which most of the people of Texas were unaware.

Some lumber company men argued privately that their companies were considering leaving one acre in five (20 percent of their land) in hardwoods. Conservationists responded that lumber companies were already getting rid of bottomland hardwoods, methodically girdling or bulldozing them, or injecting them with chemicals. There seemed to be a special war on magnolias and beech trees, though these were at the time of little market value. Conservationist skepticism was met in turn with well-financed, extensive public relations campaigns, bent on convincing the people of Texas that lumber company tree farms were chock full of deer and redolent with wildflowers. The timberfolk published busy, glossy pamphlets which proclaimed: "Planting The South's Third Forest." Whether one could call this third sterile monoculture a "forest" was debatable, conservationists countered; but there was no question that the big lumber companies (most owned in New York and Chicago) were obliterating the state's second forest.

That was the situation in 1964, and in 1970. In many respects it still is the situation. But there are differences, which point to something better than would have been thought possible in the beginning. For the sake of simplicity we will reduce the ameliorating factors to three: new parks and preserves, a new attitude among the public and also among many lumbermen, and economic forces that push low-lying lands toward conservation. We will detail these one at a time.

In 1964 there was only one sizeable "park" in the Big Thicket area: the Sam Houston National Forest. Though it was large, the purpose of a national forest, from the days of Gifford Pinchot on, was primarily that of producing a steady supply of commercial timber. Though recent debates have tended to change this emphasis toward a multiple-use doctrine which stresses biological diversity and recreation, a national forest in 1964 was no nature preserve. Through the efforts of Texas Senator Ralph W. Yarborough, 1,000 acres had been set aside in the Sam Houston forest as a kind of Big Thicket "exhibit." With only minor exceptions, that was it.

Today a different map is apparent. In October 1974 President Gerald Ford signed a bill creating the Big Thicket National Biological Preserve: the first such preserve in the history of the National Park Service. This in itself was an achievement. Parks in the nineteenth century were often preserved for their scenery: as "natural cathedrals." Now the goal was—without negating scenery—to save whole plant growth communities, the widest possible panoply of types of life: every bird, mold, mushroom, flower, insect, tree.

The preserve covered 84,550 acres. Far less than the conservationists wanted, but a victory nonetheless, it consisted of a thin 93-mile-long corridor down the Neches River from "Dam B" to Beaumont, the Jack Gore, Neches Bottom, and Beaumont units; another corridor down Little Pine Island and (Big) Pine Island Bayou from the Lance Rosier Unit to the Neches; the Beech Creek, Turkey Creek, and Hickory Creek Savannah units; the Big Sandy Unit, bordering the Alabama and Coushatta Indian Reservation on the south; the Menard Creek Corridor, reaching from the Big Sandy Unit to the Trinity River on the west; and the tiny Loblolly Unit, west of Saratoga.

It was, in one respect, an ungainly compromise. Some units stood alone; some were threaded together by stream corridors. Some units were large; some were minuscule. At some places stream corridors widened to take in meanders and oxbow lakes; at others they were razor-thin. But the Preserve contained almost every ecosystem in the Big Thicket area: baygalls, longleaf pine savannahs, palmetto palm thickets, beech forests, cypress and tupelo swamps, sphagnum bogs, shortleaf pine savannahs, insectivore bogs, bottomland hardwood forests, soaring stands of magnolias.

This was to be a beginning. Not long after the creation of the Big Thicket National Preserve (1977, in fact) the Temple-Eastex lumber company (now Temple-Inland) donated the Roy E. Larson Sandyland Sanctuary to The Nature Conservancy. Originally 2,138 acres in size, it has been enlarged by corporate donations to just under 2,400 acres. The Sandyland Sanctuary, though not part of the national preserve, completes its catalogue of major vegetation types, protecting an area of 100- to 300-feet-deep sands inhabited by xeric yucca, prickly pear and bluejack oaks, plus a sprinkling of West Texas wildflowers. Fatefully, the Larson Sanctuary also stands along Village Creek. A "ground lease" held by Temple-Inland protects the west bank of the creek here and effectively adds another 700 acres to the sanctuary.

But the addition of the Larson Sanctuary did not complete the map. In 1979 the Texas State Parks and Wildlife Department purchased an approximately 1,250-acre site, with a 2-mile frontage on Village Creek, south of the Larson Sanctuary. The site is diverse, stretching from uplands and slope forests to meander sloughs and cypress swamps. The Department plans to develop the uplands almost exclusively and only in part. Any boat ramps will be placed well away from the river otter dens and alligator slides that have been found there.

Meanwhile, over on the Trinity River, two new areas have been set aside: the 1,800-acre Davis Hill State Park and, immediately to the north, the 20,000-acre Trinity River National Wildlife Refuge. Neither of these has involved forced "taking" by government; the property of willing sellers, both are biologically rich areas. Davis Hill is a salt dome rising over 200 feet above the swampy bottomlands. The rare shadow witch orchid (*Ponthieva racemosa*), thought to be extinct in Texas, has recently been rediscovered there.

There is more. The 40-acre Dujay Sanctuary, donated to Beaumont's Lamar University, enlarges the Lance Rosier Unit, as does a 6-acre donation by the Big Thicket Association to the National Park Service. The Park Service has also recently received a 50-acre donation along the Pine Island Bayou Corridor west of its intersection with Highway 96 and a 22-acre plot on Village Creek just south of Highway 69. Formerly called the Wilfred Turner Nature Sanctuary, it was donated by the Magnolia Garden Club.

Having fought bitterly for every square inch of the Big Thicket National Preserve, conservationists are astonished now to see new lands gravitating toward the preserve, or state parks, or universities: gravitating without having to be seized, pushed, or even begged for. Why is this happening now, they ask? No one wants to belittle generous impulses or to deny that unselfish giving exists. But, realistically, conservationists have concluded that this new tide running toward conservation rests on an economic undercurrent which affects potential donors and even lumber companies—even those who have taken a dim view of conservationists.

The problem is with the low country: the bottomlands. Ecologically they are rich, diverse, and interesting. Economically they tend to be liabilities. That is, as complexes of swamps, seeps, oxbows, and meanders, they are often poor country to grow pine timber on. They may support populations of cattle (often sparse populations), or wild hogs. They may afford some sites for oil wells. The return on cattle operations in the swamp country is sometimes minimal. The owner is left to ponder whether it is worthwhile to continue paying taxes on such land—and taxes, particularly school taxes, have continued to increase.

But—it will be objected—what is to prevent the development of such land for new vacation subdivisions, fishing camps, even industrial sites? The answer is simple: floods. In the last twenty years Southeast Texas has experienced three hundred-year floods (floods so pronounced that they should only happen once in a century). No one is willing to predict how many of these will happen in the next two decades. (For that matter, every tropical storm that moves in off the Gulf offers the possibility of a nice two-hundred-year flood.) Fishing camps and cabins tend to be swept down into the Gulf of Mexico. For the bottomlands, therefore, development doesn't seem to be in the cards.

Nor should it be. The reason—as we have already noted in Chapter 5—lies in a government invention called Federal Floodplain Insurance. Originally created to afford protection for those who could not get insurance from private insurance companies, F.F.I. has become something of a monster. It has led people to build in flood-prone areas: to build there because they can get federal insurance. This not only destroys habitat for game birds and animals, for rare, scarce, or endangered species, or for the wilderness experience; it forces the federal government to pay the cost to individual homeowners to rebuild after a flood. Then, after a second flood, to pay them to rebuild again. And then, after a third . . .

In short, Federal Floodplain Insurance, however well-intentioned, turns out in many contexts to be a financial disaster. It not only leads people to build in areas that are best not developed (for many reasons, including their tendency toward inundation); it pays them to rebuild again and again. It costs too much.

Economic pressures thus suggest a continuing drift of at least the swampiest lands in Southeast Texas into environmentally protected status: into preserves, greenbelt stream corridors, scientific study areas, and parks.

This, conservationists believe, is what accounts in many cases for recent offers to donate land to the Big Thicket National Preserve. In part it also accounts for recent behavior of lumber companies. Some of these are actually beginning to set aside nature preserves on their own.

The three largest forest landowners in Southeast Texas are Temple-Inland, Champion International, and Louisiana Pacific. The largest, Temple-Inland, has virtually absorbed the former Eastex Corporation, creating a million-acre-plus complex. Louisiana Pacific has absorbed Kirby Enterprises. Champion International has absorbed both Southland Corporation and St. Regis.

At first blush the most impressive change in attitude of these massive corporate powers is evidenced in Champion International's "Special Places in the Woods Program." So far Champion has set aside ten of these, the majority of which are in the Big Thicket area. Most impressive to us is the 300-acre hardwood corridor along Battiste Creek north of Devers in Liberty County. This swampy area contains an overlap of species common to both the Lower Big Thicket and the Gulf Coastal Prairie, thus adding to the catalogue of plants already protected in the national preserve and arid sandyland sanctuary.

Other "special places" include 320 acres on Kickapoo Creek in Trinity and Polk counties; 270 acres on Dillard Creek in Walker County; the 79-acre Beech-Magnolia Canyons in Tyler County; the 40-acre Beaver Pond; the nearly 100-acre Blue Heron Rookery in Trinity County; the 145-acre Apolonia Trail in Grimes County, which mingles East and Central Texas vegetation; the 14-acre Carter Sand and Water Stop (a longleaf pine stand and spring-fed bog); a 315-acre outcrop of fossil oyster reefs in Trinity County; the wooded 50-acre Mission Señora de la Purisima Concepcion site in Angelina County; an Indian massacre site in Houston County; and a wooded area on the Neches River east of Corrigan.

These special places—which Champion International insists will be especially protected—add up to over 1,600 acres. Almost without exception they are either stream corridors or wetlands, and this bears out, to some extent, the economic-pressure-toward-conservation-in-lowlands argument mentioned above. And they are environmentally rich and interesting places. To these may be added Temple-Inland's three "environmental management zones": Wild Azalea Canyons, Scrappin Valley, and North and South Boggy Sloughs, where only selective cutting is allowed and in which, in most cases, downed trees have to be lifted out carefully rather than "skidded" through the undergrowth.

Many conservationists would retort that these are only straws in the wind—mere postage stamps against the broad backdrop of destruction waged by these three companies and their predecessors. But they do exist, and more, we are told, are planned. In 1964, when the second Big Thicket Association was formed, such things were unthinkable.

But something still more pervasive is happening: a shift in policy toward clearcutting. In 1991 Louisiana Pacific publicly renounced clearcutting in California. On its over 650,000 Texas acres this corporation has practiced "selective harvesting" tree by tree rather than whole-forest removal. Champion International, though still clearcutting, is beginning to leave straggles of hardwood trees along creeks and ravines, and plans to widen such minimal corridors in the future.

The shift is clearest in the case of the largest landowner, Temple-Inland. There is now a steady demand for furniture-grade hardwood, a demand which can hardly be met by pulp pine plantations. Temple-Inland has thus established a Best-Use Policy, which proposes to let bottomland hardwoods grow for forty or even fifty years before harvesting them. In the moist reaches of Southeast Texas a forty- to fifty-year-old forest is well developed indeed. As Temple-Inland views the future, hunters, birdwatchers, fishermen, and research biologists will be able to look forward to a vast web of hardwood forests along area streams throughout the corporation's 1,000,000-plus acres. These hardwoods will, when the time comes, be clearcut. But such clearcuts, Temple-Inland tells us, will average 30 acres, and will be narrow and winding: a boon to wildlife, which profits from the "edge effects" such smaller, thinner clearcuts will provide.

It is a little over thirty years since a handful of local people met in a church in Saratoga to begin a regional conservation movement. The results are clear on a map of the Big Thicket region. Where once there were no nature preserves, now there are many; where once nothing—virtually nothing at all—was protected, now much is: a national biological preserve, an arid sandyland sanctuary, two state parks, a national wildlife refuge, over a dozen Special Places in the Woods, with more scheduled. None of those who founded the Big Thicket Association could have believed that this was possible.

Equally important—some would say even more important in the long run—is the change in attitudes and practices by lumber companies. Most important of these is the budding willingness of the three major corporations to protect hardwood bottomlands. If this willingness is continued, then some semblance of original wilderness conditions can remain. At least, a naturally interconnected web of hardwoods following the area's many waterways would protect stream water quality and allow for circulation of animal—and even plant—species. It would allow for the continued existence of a multitude of living things which otherwise would cease to be multitudes, and even to exist. It would allow for some continuation of the native integument: the tangle of overstory and understory, richness and diversity, owl and heron and fern and wild swamp azalea.

Now there is hope that a system of stream corridors and natural preserves (units, sanctuaries), whether managed by state, federal, or private sources, will sustain a significant portion of a region's ecology—without damage to its economy. Unity, stability, and beauty thus are embodied in a new approach to the land—one which was not originally planned, but which like Topsy, just grew.

What has happened in Southeast Texas—more hopefully, what is still happening and needs to continue happening—is not unique. The still faltering drive to turn the forks of the Trinity River in the Dallas–Fort Worth metroplex into a system of parks and greenbelts is similar enough to the situation in Southeast Texas to bear mention. It even contains a proposed large "unit" along the stream corridor: the Great Trinity Forest. If completed it would be a boon to the metroplex, and a nationally recognized "signature" for the entire region. Worth mentioning, too, are efforts to protect and connect areas along the lower Rio Grande (the "Valley"), so as to provide habitat for rare, scarce, and endangered species there. So are suggested projects for protecting the character of the Texas Hill Country. In all of this, we hasten to point out, there are no plans to take property from unwilling sellers, eject people from their homes, or cripple regional economies. There are a lot of ways to save an ecology. We just have to be creative enough to see how to do it without making a frontal assault on landowners, homeowners, and the general productivity.

The implications of this situation and this approach, in fact, point far beyond the borders of the Lone Star State. We have seen maps of the Amazon Basin which suggest a similar complex of protected stream corridors and wilderness preserves as a way of dealing with surging development. But it is not necessary to go as far as Amazonia to find applications for the stream corridor and sanctuary approach. Vast areas of the American South are similar enough in vegetation and topography to utilize the patterns developing in Southeast Texas.

*Tiquesha Roberson playing in her
yard abutting Waste Management,
Inc., Municipal Landfill, Ferris.*

7

A CONCLUSION

There is more than one way to look at a state—or a country, or a world—and there is more than one way to look at ethics. Those familiar with academic philosophy are all too well aware of the long-standing debates and endless discussions that mark the history of this field. Such persons would point out that our presentation of Leopold's land ethics fails to carefully distinguish "deontological" (duty-based) from "consequentialist" (result-based) ethics, that it does not demarcate either of these from a "contextualist" (situation-based) approach. They would probably insist that, in any case, we commit the "naturalistic fallacy" (by deducing a series of "oughts" from a bunch of environmental "facts").

While conceding that such questions are interesting and worth considering, we think that such critics miss an important—*the* most important—point. We agree with Leopold that the fundamental transformations of human valuing, which have broadened and deepened our basic ethical horizons, have not taken place in a historical and social vacuum. They have happened in situations of crisis: in contexts where old cultural assumptions and values no longer meet human needs, no longer fit a changed situation. The settling-down of humankind from a hunting-gathering into an agricultural mode of life was one of these. The leap from an agricultural to an industrial civilization was another. The collision of an industrial civilization with its physical environment is another still. This is our present crisis.

Some will argue that such crises mark nothing more than changed social and technological situations, without long-term ethical or moral implications. Like Leopold, we disagree. Really new, challenging, threatening situations from which it is impossible for humankind to withdraw are precisely the crucibles in which new moral values and vistas are forged. Compared to these, the debates of academic philosophers seem strangely abstract.

It could be argued that, granted the truth of Leopold's observation that profound transformations in ethics happen in the midst of profound crises in human existence, it does not follow that his land ethic is the ultimate, complete, and final response to the present environmental situation. We make no claims that it is. We choose Leopold because his ideas are clear, applicable, plausible, and based on a lifetime of experience with nature and humankind's interaction with nature. He made no claims to have brought down a set of engraved tablets from heaven. His ideas were growing and changing even as he wrote them, and would have grown further had he lived. Even so, they are to the point. We agree with him that our new, virtually unheralded situation calls for a viewpoint that takes nature seriously, and hence values it. And we agree that wholeness, stability, and beauty are realistic benchmarks to bear in mind in thinking about the natural world and what one would wish it to become: or remain.

That this might have something to do with Texas, or any other state—that it might have a great deal to do with the world, humanity, and what both might become—seems clear enough. But we have tried to make it clearer by an appeal to facts. What has happened in one particular case—the Lone Star State? What is now happening there, and with what results? We have tried to spell this out, attempting in the process to obliterate the false picture of Texas as still a wide-open frontier with unlimited resources ready for the taking or—much the same thing—a virgin landscape virtually untouched by human hands. These images are false. The belief that they are true does great harm.

The fact that the frontier, with its easy expectation of surplus, is over is obvious to most observers. But it is not obvious to most Texans, for whom frontier still seems the natural order of things. What we have pointed out above is true: from the 1820s through the 1950s Texas remained a frontier. If the land frontier dwindled and passed out of existence circa 1900, the raw materials frontier continued for another half-century. That this frontier, too, has passed seems *wrong* to traditional Texans: wrong, and contrary to the natural order of things. But the realization that this is so—that the old roughshod frontier is over—is necessary to any realistic assessment of the future. Put rhetorically: it is the foundation of both economic and ecological sustainability.

So we have tried to pile on the facts, to provide a realistic picture of our present situation. At the forefront are the Giant Slurbs, the very symbol of this book. At the end of World War II, these did not exist. Now they stretch twofold across the post oaks, the blackland prairie, the Piney Woods, and are beginning, at least, to connect Dallas to Galveston, Fort Worth to San Antonio. Each represents millions of people, people requiring fuel, fiber, space, food, transportation; each produces inevitable pollution; each increasingly covers over prime farm, cattle, and timber land. Within a generation the dotted lines will be solid, the spaces will be filled. It would seem strange to call this a frontier. As in Southern California and the urban Northeast, this is the opposite of a frontier. It is full land, overflowing with people, cramped for resources.

But move away from the Giant Slurbs to the High Plains, to what geographers call America's "Empty Quadrant." Here the problem is not too many people: it is too little water. Or, inversely, it is water too much and too rapidly pumped. The methods which have led to a boom in "food and fiber" production on the Texas High Plains are leading to a serious retrenching of the boom, even, according to many observers, an eventual conversion back to dry land farming and ranching. Faced with the inevitable, High Plains agriculturalists have begun to hoard water, to find ways to ration its use, to protect the resource they once used so casually. But frontier abundance is gone. How long larger-scale irrigated agriculture can last in the land above the Caprock is anyone's guess.

But move away from the dry, high Caprock to the humid, subtropical Gulf. Here, too, the news is less than pleasant. Texas began the century with vast, unspoiled beaches, seemingly unlimited fisheries, and clean saltwater stretching toward endless horizons. Virtually untouched by urban or industrial development, the Coastal Zone beckoned as another seemingly inexhaustible resource. But large areas of this resource are now developed, either for industry or for beachfront and bayfront recreation. No one can say how much of the new housing will last out the next large hurricane. But anyone familiar with the situation can say that Lavaca Bay is contaminated with methyl mercury, and that its once abundant fisheries are closed, both to the private and to the commercial fishermen. And anyone can add that tidal action is slowly moving these pollutants toward nearby Matagorda Bay, and toward the Gulf. Couple this with the fact that Galveston

Bay (Texas' largest bay and the nation's seventh largest) receives 60 percent of the state's total water pollution, and once again the moral is clear. The state's Coastal Zone is already damaged. In two generations it has passed from a frontier to a limited, no longer abundant resource.

Almost anywhere one puts one's finger down on the map of Texas, then, the story is the same. In virtually every county—not just on the High Plains—the underground water table is dropping, often in the fifties and hundreds of feet. But if underground water resources are dwindling, few additional sites are available for storing surface water. Similarly, though many still live who have vivid memories of the oil boom of the 1930s and '40s, not only water is dwindling underground. The high old times of big new oil finds are over in the Lone Star State. One might as well hope for a major gold rush. With luck, deep basin drilling will tap new sources of natural gas. But never again will oil—or even natural gas—fuel the major part of Texas' economy.

There is no need to go on and on. We have already belabored these and other negative points—endangered species, toxic dumps, habitat loss. Together they spell the end of a boom based primarily on raw materials, natural resources. The future suggests a very different kind of economy, in which the state will have to live by its brains, so to speak: exploiting new technologies, merchandizing, developing new markets, advertising. It makes sense to us that as the economy shifts, so should our approach to the land and its ecologies. The old, roughshod, let-the-devil-take-the-hindmost approach—to put it bluntly—is too expensive. It always was. But with abundant resources and a small population (1 million in 1900 compared to 17.6 million now), it was possible in the past to proceed full speed ahead in exploiting the land without worrying about the consequences. Today this is no longer so. By undercutting the land, we now jeopardize our own future.

There are some who, though they grant the truth of what is said here, argue that the solution lies in two very simple acts: (1) Pass stringent laws. (2) Enforce them (and fine the miscreants or put them in jail). While it is clear that government and legal systems have a role to play in all human affairs, we do not think that by themselves they provide the solution. Laws that are not believed in by a sizeable portion of a community are not passed; or if passed, they are not enforced. Not every law, enforced or not, is a good law; and even the best of laws are general, and have to be interpreted to "fit" particular circumstances. We believe that the best, the most effective, situation involves actual human beings who *care* about nature, who make the effort to understand it, and who therefore will apply that understanding to the world. This requires more and better than draconic legal codes. It requires an ethic, both incarnate in individuals and broadly shared by a community.

Suppose, for the sake of argument, that some ethic like Leopold's had been broadly shared by Texans during the state's long frontier experience.

No doubt the American Southwest—to take only one example—would have developed more slowly. To take nature seriously and (much the same thing) to think about its future along with the human future is to be patient, and careful. It is not, however, to be paralyzed. As we have repeatedly emphasized, a land ethic does not take away human rights to live upon the land. How would this be possible for a viewpoint which includes human beings and all other creatures as co-members of a common community?

The somewhat slower pace of development—its very thoughtfulness— would, however, have produced results both economically and ecologically beneficial. Suppose the waters of the Ogallala Aquifer had been used more carefully and more slowly? Consideration for the long-term stability of this system would have meant that today there would be more, not less underground water, and that irrigated agriculture on the Texas High Plains would last longer—perhaps indefinitely. Likewise for the state's Coastal Zone. Concern for the integrity and stability of the Gulf Coast would not have meant building a fence around it so that Galveston, Rockport, and Corpus Christi would not exist. But it would have precluded letting over 200,000 people live on land around Houston-Galveston that is well within reach of the surge tide of strong hurricanes: 200,000 people who Civil Defense experts are convinced cannot all be moved out before the center of a really powerful hurricane arrives. Similarly, the wide acceptance of a land ethic would have prevented the pollution of Lavaca Bay, with the potential also for the destruction of Laguna Madre. The issue of beauty counts here, too. A polluted, garbage-strewn beach is no more beautiful than a fish kill. Clean saltwater smells good and sparkles in the morning sun. But it also supports fisheries once worth $200,000,000 a year and tourism worth billions.

Likewise for the Woodlands. Since the chapter on the Big Thicket was written, a precedent-setting agreement between Champion International and the Texas State Parks and Wildlife Department has guaranteed that 50,000 acres of bottomland owned by the corporation—much of it in the Big Thicket region—will be jointly managed by the company and the state agency to ensure the greatest richness and diversity of species in the area. This arrangement has been entered into freely by both parties. It is not a shotgun wedding decreed by Evil Government. It is a farsighted act entered into by both parties and, we can hope, one to the advantage of both: and to everyone.

But let us suppose that the timbering of the state's forest region had been done on the basis of a shared environmental ethic, instead of the odd mixture of nature romanticism and ruthless calculation that typified even the best foresters of the time—including the young Leopold. The early lumbermen *cut everything*, and they *planted nothing*. The over 600,000 acres of national forest in the state is precisely a function of the ruins that were left—ruined, cutover lands more stump than tree, eroded and well nigh worthless. In the 1930s the federal government came in to reclaim tracts that no one wanted, proving that virtual moonscapes could again become productive. But if even modest attempts to protect the land and to replant it had taken place, the federal presence so resented by the forest products industries would never have been called for.

But there is more to it than this. If even a few ancient groves of hardwoods or longleaf pines had been saved by the early lumbermen, they would today be regarded as marvels of nature and gems of the American South. If the slightest effort had been made to leave a few scattered trees as sentinels to reseed their kind, or if anyone had tried to cut so as not to fragment the forest habitat, perhaps today we would still have the (now extinct) ivory-billed woodpecker with us and the red-cockaded woodpecker would not be an endangered species. Purebred Texas red wolves would still range the backwoods and the brown bear would still be common in the tangled bottomlands.

The main thrust of this book, however, is not backwards but forwards. We face the past with evident regrets; how should we face the future? In general, we believe, hope will accomplish more than despair. The land ethic provides a basis for an active approach to our problems: an approach which can be positive, first, because it admits that problems exist and, second, because it suggests what is required to solve them. To talk about the integrity, the beauty, and the stability of natural communities may be to talk in general. But it is not to talk vacuous generalities. To engage in thoughtless habitat fragmentation is, unless island biogeography is a hallucination, to lose species of every kind, perhaps irreversibly. There are reasons to be concerned about the "integrity" of ecosystems. To talk about the stability of nature is not to specify in each case what this stability will consist of. That, however, begins to become apparent when one gets down to cases. The stability of prairies is lost if they are perpetually overgrazed in the face of inevitable periodic droughts.

This is only to say that a land ethic involves us in our natural world and orients us toward fruitful ways of living in it without wrecking it. Beyond this, philosophy and ethics cannot go. They orient us in general, fruitful ways. Experience, common sense, and the natural and social sciences must fill in the details. No philosophy can deduce the particulars of our experience.

Some further points must be made before closing off this study. The first concerns the relations between world and national trends and those which concern us locally or regionally. The second involves economic factors.

The base axiom of all environmentalism is: Everything is connected to everything. Not in the same degree (some things are only tangentially or minimally related); and not always in the same way (sometimes, for example, there is negative feedback, sometimes positive); but always. Insecticides sprayed over Valley View, Texas, find their way eventually to Galveston Bay, over 250 river miles away. The rise of temperature by 1° Fahrenheit per annum in Texas and New Mexico affects the relict evergreen forests on the crest of the Guadalupe Mountains and the tidal flats near Brownsville. The plume from a toxic metal smelter can weaken forests for 100 miles downwind, and an improved antipollution technology, conversely, can strengthen them.

If such things are true (they are easy to prove), then though there are good reasons to concentrate on the land ethics of a region, a state, or a locale, there is no justification for treating any of these as if they existed in splendid isolation. The Texas flag displays a *lone star*; but the state is inextricably affected by, and affects, myriad factors in its environment. Just as each of us has an ecological "footprint," so does the state. And also, the state can be stepped on from outside.

It is important, therefore, to stress the way in which, for example, global warming—a worldwide phenomenon by definition—would affect the state. Suppose that world temperature increased by 5–6° Fahrenheit annually: a high figure, but not the "worst-case scenario." The Gulf, like all the world's oceans, would then rise by around 6 feet. How many tens of thousands more people would be put within reach of hurricane flood tides? How many subdivisions in Galveston or Baytown or Rockport would be underwater at high tide? At even half that figure large parts of Galveston Island, and all of the Gulf barrier islands, would disappear.

Or, consider the impact on climate. The hottest temperature ever measured in Texas was 120°: near Seymour, in the 1920s. This anomaly, with a 5–6° rise in annual mean temperature, would become the norm in

Dallas–Fort Worth, which could see 120° days ten to fourteen times every summer. One-hundred-degree days would be declared cool. Increased water evaporation ratios and decreased rainfall under such circumstances would have a grim impact on farmers, ranchers, and forest products industries. Texas' already tightened water budget would be stretched past the breaking point.

We would like to believe that this prospect is only a hallucination—a mirage projected on the basis of insufficient data. But it appears, on the best evidence we can find, to be more than a mirage. On the basis of this evidence, at least two conclusions seem inescapable. No part of the planet is secure from effects on the planet generally, whether from acid rain, global warming, ozone holes, or sheer climate destabilization. World environmental changes affect us as surely as does a globalized world economy. And (the second point) a sane response to this fact would seem to be caution: caution, and a persistent attempt to reduce our greenhouse gas production without dismembering our economy in the process. Texans, who produce more CO_2 emissions than the citizens of any other state in the country, might do well to reflect on these facts: and see what might be done about them.

Which brings us, as nearly everything sooner or later does, to economics. It is precisely here that we believe environmentalism in general and land ethics in particular have been misunderstood. The goal of land ethics is certainly the reform of economic factors which disguise the real costs of doing business. A land ethics approach does not attempt to abolish, or to enfeeble, a system of free markets. It does attempt to plug some of the leaks in free market plumbing. But it also attempts to bring environmentalists to think more realistically about economics and ecology.

We will conclude by trying to drive home three points. The first is, contrary to what you are likely to hear, that to clean up your environment is not necessarily to risk your economy. It may well be a plus. The second is that current ways of measuring environmental costs need to be changed. The hidden costs are kept hidden. They need to be brought out into the open. The third is that we haven't even begun to think about bringing economics and ecology together. To begin thinking in this direction is, of course, to look for the middle ground, where disparate views can be brought together. But it is also to look for solutions we have not even considered.

We have only begun to consider what is involved in making a marriage of the green dollar and the green earth. We know that it will be a marriage made not in heaven, but here on earth. And we know that as in any real marriage, there will have to be a lot of rethinking and reflecting—and some concessions—on both sides. We urge that in contemplating such a union, the land ethic provides a practical, wise, intelligible guide.

The Lone Star State has been blessed with rich resources, great pride, and an industrious people capable of taking advantage of what it has. There is no reason to belittle what has been done. But if it is to remain a place of lush prairies, breathable air, deep woods; of available waters and fishable streams, and clean beaches and abundant game: then many things will have to change. This is a real challenge. All pessimisms to the contrary, we think the challenge can be met.

BIBLIOGRAPHY

Almanza, Susan R., Antonio Díaz, Mary E. Kelly, and Mary Sanger. 1993. *Toxics in Texas and Their Impact on Communities of Color*. Austin: Texas Center for Policy Studies.

Baccus, J. T., ed. 1982. *Texas Wildlife Resources and Land Use*. Austin: Texas Chapter, The Wildlife Society.

Beamish, Rita. 1993. "Minorities Push 'Environmental Justice.'" *Dallas Morning News* (December 20):36A.

Bormann, F. H., and S. R. Kellert, eds. 1992. *Ecology, Economics, Ethics: The Broken Circle*. New Haven, Conn.: Yale University Press.

Bowman, Jean A. 1993. "The Rio Grande: A Confluence of Waters, Nations and Cultures." *Texas Water Resources* 19(2):1–5.

Brammer, B. L. 1986. *The Gay Place*. New York: Vintage Books.

Bryan, K., T. Gallucci, G. Lasley, and D. H. Riskind. 1991. *A Checklist of Texas Birds*. Austin: Texas Parks and Wildlife Department.

Bullard, Robert D. 1990. *Dumping in Dixie: Race, Class, and Environmental Quality*. San Francisco: Westview Press.

Caldwell, Lynton Keith, and Kristin Shrader-Frechette. 1993. *Policy for Land: Law and Ethics*. Lanham, Md.: Rowman & Littlefield.

Callicott, J. Baird, ed. 1987. *Companion to "A Sand County Almanac": Interpretive and Critical Essays*. Madison: University of Wisconsin Press.

Callicott, J. Baird. 1989. *In Defense of the Land Ethic: Essays in Environmental Philosophy*. Albany: State University of New York Press.

Cobb, Clifford W. 1989. "The Index of Sustainable Economic Welfare," in Daly and Cobb 1989, *For the Common Good.*

Colborn, Theo, Dianne Dumanoski, and John Peterson Myers. 1996. *Our Stolen Future: Are We Threatening Our Fertility, Intelligence, and Survival?—A Scientific Detective Story.* New York: Dutton.

Collection: Series 9/25/10, Leopold Papers, University of Wisconsin–Madison Archives.

Correll, Donovan S. 1971. "Statement of Donovan S. Correll, Texas Research Institute." *Hearing before the Subcommittee on National Parks and Recreation of the Committee on Interior and Insular Affairs, United States Senate (Beaumont, Texas, June 12, 1970).* Washington, D.C.: U.S. Government Printing Office.

Corson, W. 1990. *Global Ecological Handbook.* Boston: Beacon Press.

Costanza, Robert, ed. 1992. *Ecological Economics: The Science and Management of Sustainability.* New York: Columbia University Press.

Daly, Herman E. 1991. *Steady-State Economics: Second Edition with New Essays.* Washington, D.C.: Island Press.

———. 1994. "Operationalizing Sustainable Development by Investing in Natural Capital," in Jansson et al. 1994, *Investing in Natural Capital.*

———, and John B. Cobb, Jr. 1989. *For the Common Good: Redirecting the Economy toward Community, the Environment, and a Sustainable Future.* Boston: Beacon Press.

Dixon, J. R. 1987. *Amphibians and Reptiles of Texas: With Keys, Taxonomic Synopses, Bibliography, and Distribution Maps.* College Station: Texas A. & M. University Press.

Eckhardt, Bob. 1994. "Review of *The Big Thicket: An Ecological Reevaluation*, by Pete A. Y. Gunter." *Texas Books in Review* 14(4):17–18.

Ehrlich, Paul R. 1968. *The Population Bomb.* New York: Ballantine.

———, and Anne H. Ehrlich. 1990. *The Population Explosion.* New York: Simon & Schuster.

Ekins, Paul, Mayer Hillman, and Robert Hutchison. 1992. *The Gaia Atlas of Green Economics.* New York: Anchor Books.

Feeny, Paul, and Thomas Eisner. 1972. "Statement of Dr. Paul Feeny; Accompanied by Thomas Eisner, *Ad Hoc* Committee to Save the Big Thicket, Cornell University." *Hearing before the Subcommittee on National Parks and Recreation of the Committee on Interior and Insular Affairs (Beaumont, Texas, June 10, 1972).* Washington, D.C.: U.S. Government Printing Office.

Firor, John. 1990. *The Changing Atmosphere: A Global Challenge.* New Haven, Conn.: Yale University Press.

Flader, Susan. 1974. *Thinking Like a Mountain: Aldo Leopold and the Evolution of an Ecological Attitude toward Deer, Wolves, and Forests.* Columbia: University of Missouri Press.

Georgescu-Roegen, Nicholas. 1971. *The Entropy Law and the Economic Process.* Cambridge, Mass.: Harvard University Press.

Glanz, James. 1995. "Erosion Study Finds High Price for Forgotten Menace." *Science* 267:1088.

Glasser, Harold, and Paul P. Craig. 1994. "Towards Biogeophysically Based 'Green Accounts.'" *Trumpeter* 11(2):95–102.

Glenn, Jim. 1992. "The State of Garbage in America." *BioCycle* 33(4):46–51.

Goldfarb, William. 1992. "Groundwater: The Buried Life," in Bormann and Kellert, eds., 1992, *Ecology, Economics, Ethics.*

Goldsteen, Joel B. 1993. *Danger All Around: Waste Storage Crisis on the Texas and Louisiana Gulf Coast.* Austin: University of Texas Press.

Graves, J. 1960. *Goodbye to a River.* Austin: Texas Monthly Press.

———. 1974. *Hard Scrabble: Observations on a Patch of Land.* Austin: Texas Monthly Press.

Gunter, Pete A. Y. 1971. *The Big Thicket: A Challenge for Conservation.* Austin: Jenkins.

———. 1993. *The Big Thicket: An Ecological Reevaluation.* Denton: University of North Texas Press.

Hardin, Garrett. 1968. "The Tragedy of the Commons." *Science* 162:1243–1248.

———. 1993. *Living within Limits: Ecology, Economics, and Population Taboos.* New York: Oxford University Press.

Hatch, S. L., K. N. Gandhi, and L. E. Brown. 1990. *Checklist of the Vascular Plants of Texas.* College Station: Texas Agricultural Experiment Station.

Hawken, Paul. 1993. *The Ecology of Commerce.* New York: HarperCollins.

Hubbs, C., R. J. Edwards, and G. P. Garrett. 1991. "An Annotated Checklist of the Freshwater Fishes of Texas, with Keys to Identification of Species." *Texas Journal of Science*, Suppl. 43(4):1–56.

Jansson, AnnMari, et al., eds. 1994. *Investing in Natural Capital: The Ecological Economics Approach to Sustainability.* Washington, D.C.: Island Press.

Johnston, R. J. 1989. *Environmental Problems: Nature, Economy and State.* London, England: Belhaven Press.

Jones, J. K., Jr., and C. Jones. 1992. "Revised Checklist of Recent Land Mammals of Texas, with Annotations." *Texas Journal of Science* 44(1):54–74.

Kessler, Barbara. 1993. "TU Electric to Pay Fine for Nuclear Plant Spill." *Dallas Morning News* (December 31):27A.

LaFreniere, Gilbert. 1993. "Land-Use Planning and the Land Ethic." *Trumpeter* 10(2):59–62.

Leopold, Aldo. 1970. *A Sand County Almanac: With Essays on Conservation from Round River.* San Francisco: Sierra Club Books. Orig. pub. 1949, Oxford University Press.

———. 1986. *Game Management.* Madison: University of Wisconsin Press. Orig. pub. 1933, Charles Scribner's Sons.

———. 1992. *The River of the Mother of God and Other Essays by Aldo Leopold*, ed. Susan L. Flader and J. Baird Callicott. Madison: University of Wisconsin Press.

———. n.d. *See* Collection: Series 9/25/10.

Linthicum, Leslie. 1996. "Texas Farmers Fight Underground Drought." *Albuquerque Journal* (May 16):A1, A6.

Loehr, Raymond. 1991. "What Raised the Issue?" *EPA Journal* (March/April):6–12.

McCloskey, Donald N. 1985. *The Rhetoric of Economics*. Madison: University of Wisconsin Press.

Machado, Sheila, and Rick Piltz. 1988. *Reducing the Rate of Global Warming: The States' Role*. Washington, D.C.: Renew America.

McLeod, Claude A. 1967. *The Big Thicket of East Texas*. Huntsville, Tex.: Sam Houston Press.

———. 1970. "The Big Thicket Forest of East Texas." *Texas Journal of Science* 23(2):221–233.

McMurtry, Larry. 1968. *In a Narrow Grave*. Austin: Encino Press.

MacNeil, Jim, Peter Winsemius, and Taizo Yakushiji. 1992. *Beyond Interdependence: The Meshing of the World's Economy and the Earth's Ecology*. New York: Oxford University Press.

Marinelli, Janet. 1990. "After the Flush: The Next Generation." *Garbage* 2(1):24–35.

Mayr, Ernst. 1982. *The Growth of Biological Thought: Diversity, Evolution, and Inheritance*. Cambridge, Mass.: Harvard University Press.

Meine, Curt. 1988. *Aldo Leopold: His Life and Work*. Madison: University of Wisconsin Press.

———. 1992. "The Utility of Preservation and the Preservation of Utility: Leopold's Fine Line," in Oelschlaeger, ed., 1992, *The Wilderness Condition*.

Meyer, Stephen M. 1992. "Environmentalism and Economic Prosperity: Testing the Environmental Impact Hypothesis." Cambridge, Mass.: MIT Project on Environmental Politics and Policy.

———. 1993. "Environmentalism and Economic Prosperity: An Update." Cambridge, Mass.: MIT Project on Environmental Politics and Policy.

———. (in press). *Environmentalism and Economic Prosperity*. Cambridge, Mass.: MIT Press.

Moore, Curtis. 1995. "Green Revolution in the Making." *Sierra* (January–February):50–52, 126–130.

———, and Alan Miller. 1994. *Green Gold: Japan, Germany, the United States, and the Race for Environmental Technology*. Boston: Beacon Press.

n.a. 1993. "Warning Toxic Texas: Locked Horns over Lavaca." *Texas Shores* (Winter).

National Commission on the Environment. 1993. *Choosing a Sustainable Future: The Report of the National Commission on the Environment*. Washington, D.C.: Island Press.

North, Gerald R., Jurgen Schmandt, and Judith Clarkson. 1995. *The Impact of Global Warming on Texas: A Report of the Task Force on Climate Change*. Austin: University of Texas Press.

Odum, Eugene P. 1993. *Ecology and Our Endangered Life Support Systems*, 2d ed. Sunderland, Mass.: Sinauer.

Oelschlaeger, Max. 1991. *The Idea of Wilderness: From Prehistory to the Age of Ecology*. New Haven, Conn.: Yale University Press.

———. 1992. *After Earth Day: Continuing the Conservation Effort*. Denton: University of North Texas Press.

———, ed. 1992. *The Wilderness Condition: Essays on Environment and Civilization*. San Francisco: Sierra Club Books.

———. 1994. *Caring for Creation: An Ecumenical Approach to the Environmental Crisis*. New Haven, Conn.: Yale University Press.

Pimentel, David, et al. 1995. "Environmental and Economic Costs of Soil Erosion and Conservation Benefits." *Science* 267:1117–1122.

Prigogine, Ilya, and Isabelle Stengers. 1984. *Order Out of Chaos: Man's New Dialogue with Nature*. New York: Bantam.

Rees, William E., and Mathis Wackernagel. 1994. "Ecological Footprints and Appropriate Carrying Capacity: Measuring the Natural Capital Requirements of the Human Economy," in Jansson et al., 1994, *Investing in Natural Capital*.

Sagoff, Mark. 1988. *The Economy of the Earth: Philosophy, Law, and the Environment*. New York: Cambridge University Press.

Schmidheiny, Stephan. 1992. *Changing Course: Report of the World Business Council on Sustainable Development*. Cambridge, Mass.: MIT Press.

Spearing, Darwin. 1991. *Roadside Geology of Texas*. Missoula, Mont.: Mountain Press Publishing Company.

State of Texas Environmental Priorities Project. 1996. "State of Texas Environmental Priorities Project: Final Report" (Draft Copy). Austin: STEPP.

Stewart, Sharon. 1992. *Toxic Tour of Texas*. Houston.

Sturzl, Frank J. 1991. "A Necessary Tyranny: How Environmental Programs Threaten to Bankrupt Cities and How Common Sense Became Heresy." *Texas Town and City* (July):1.

Texas Center for Policy Studies. 1995. *Texas Environmental Almanac*. Austin: Texas Center for Policy Studies.

Texas Clean Water Council. 1992. *Texas Water Council Recommendations to the Texas Water Commission*. Austin: Texas Water Commission.

Texas Comptroller of Public Accounts. 1991. "Texas at Risk." *Fiscal Notes* (August):12.

———. 1993. "The Environment," in *Forces of Change: Shaping the Future of Texas* (Vol. II, Pt. 1). Austin: State of Texas.

Texas Department of Water Resources. 1979. *Groundwater Availability in Texas, Estimates and Projects through 2030*. Austin: TDWR.

United Nations. 1992. *Agenda 21: Programme of Action for Sustainable Development*. New York: United Nations Department of Public Information.

U.S. Environmental Protection Agency. 1991. *Protecting the Nation's Ground Water: EPA's Strategy for the 1990s*. Washington, D.C.: USEPA.

———. 1992a. *Environmental Equity: Reducing Risk for All Communities*. Washington, D.C.: USEPA.

————. 1992b. *EPA Summary: Environmental Plan for the Mexican-U.S. Border Area (First Stage, 1992–1994)*. Washington, D.C.: USEPA.

U.S. National Park Service. 1967. "Proposed Big Thicket National Monument, Texas; A Study of Alternatives." Washington, D.C.: National Park Service.

Webb, Walter Prescott. 1953. *The Great Frontier: An Interpretation of World History since Columbus*. London, England: Seeker and Warburg.

White, Lynn, Jr. 1967. "The Historical Roots of Our Ecologic Crisis." *Science* 155: 1203–1207.

Wigley, T. M. L., and S. C. B. Raper. 1992. "Implications for Climate and Sea Level of Revised IPCC Emissions Scenarios." *Nature* 357:293–300.

Wilson, Edward O. 1992. *The Diversity of Life*. Cambridge, Mass.: The Belknap Press of Harvard University Press.

Wooldridge, J. C. 1982. "Urban Growth and Wilderness Values in Texas," in Baccus, ed., 1982, *Texas Wildlife Resources and Land Use*.

World Commission on Environment and Development. 1987. *Our Common Future*. New York: Oxford University Press.

INDEX

Acid rain, 54, 93, 136
AEC, 58
Africa, 38–39
Agenda 21, 85–86, 89, 93, 143. *See also* Sustainable development; UNCED
AIDS, 39
Air pollution, 38, 66–68, 74, 85, 94. *See also* Acid rain; Global warming; Greenhouse gases; Ozone depletion; Suspended particulates
Air quality, 31, 33, 37, 54, 76, 85, 92–93
Alabama and Coushatta Indian Reservation, 115, 122
Alaska, 14, 78, 98
Alligators, xv, 116
Alvin, 58
Amarillo, 28, 50, 57
Amazon Basin, 127. *See also* Rainforests
American Association for the Advancement of Science, 89
American Chemical Society, 48

American eagle, 88
American Midwest, 11
American South, 127, 134
American Southwest, 13, 133
Amphibians, xi, 53–54, 140
Anencephaly, 48
Angelina County, 125
Anhingas, 119
Anthropogenic disturbance, 50, 53–56
Anti-intellectualism, xiv, 25
Apache National Forest, 3
Apolonia Trail, 125
Appalachian Region, 110
Aquifers, 45, 52, 64, 70, 73, 99. *See also* Edwards Aquifer; Ogallala Aquifer
Aransas National Wildlife Refuge, 22
Arizona, 3–4, 92
Arkansas, 44
Arroyo Hondo, 108
Athens, 15
Atomic Energy Commission, 58

Austin: and development, 86; and geography, 20, 22, 52; and politics, 17, 46; and pollution, 33; as urban area, 34
Austin Chalk, 70

Bacteria, 39, 50
Barrier Islands, xiv, 27, 36, 100, 135
Barton Springs, 86
Batson, 25, 109
Battiste Creek, 125
Baygall, 115, 117, 122
Bayport, 44
Baytown, 135
Bears, xv, 4, 26, 125
Beaumont, 22, 109, 111, 115, 122–123
Beauty: as criterion for judgment, 11, 14–17, 35–36, 75; and the land, xii, xiii, 82; and the market, 105; as natural, 6, 130; protection of, 94, 98, 101, 118, 127, 133–134; as a value to be preserved, 67. *See also* Land ethics
Beauty strips, 15, 26
Beaver, 119, 125
Beech Creek Unit, 122
Beech-Magnolia Canyons, 125
Beech trees, 117, 121
Bhopal, India, 88
Big Bend National Park, xi, 22, 54
Big Sandy Unit, 122
Big Thicket: as exemplary conservation site, xv; as impacted by human activity, 12, 26, 49, 52; and Leopold, vii; maps, 112–113; mentioned, 101; and National Biological Preserve, 120–123, 125–126, 133; photograph of, 106; recovery of, 107–112, 114–117, 119
Big Thicket Association, 114, 123
Big Thicket National Park, 114, 119
Biodiversity, 37, 39, 59; as conservation issue, xiv; as ecological risk, 33; as global issue, 52–53; and population growth, xii; as Texas issue, 53–54; and wilderness habitat, 102
Bioregions, 21, 23, 33–34
Biosystem services, 39, 60, 68, 72–73
Bird species, 111
Bitterns, 119
Blue Angel Program, 93
Blue heron, 125
Bluejack oak, 110
Boggy sloughs, 125
Booms, 24–25, 32, 112. *See also* Cattle; Cotton; Irrigated agriculture; Oil; Timber
Boomtowns, 109
Botanists, 111
Bottomlands, 12, 20, 33, 36, 52, 102, 121, 123–124
Brammer, Billy Lee, 19, 139
Brazos River, 25, 34–35, 41, 58, 121
Brownsville, xiii, 20, 135
Brush Country, 21, 23, 25
Bull snakes, 117
Bunton, Lucius, 46
Burger King, 96
Burkburnett, 25

CAFE, 97
California, 19, 44, 131; and clearcutting, 126; compared to Texas, x, 14, 23, 39, 45, 50, 53, 74; and land-use law, 77
Canyon, 22, 27, 117
Caprock, the, 21, 131. *See also* High Plains; Panhandle
Carbon cycle, 54–55, 64–65, 68, 90
Carbon dioxide (CO_2), x, 34, 54–56, 58, 68, 72, 74, 87, 90, 97
Carbon monoxide, 54
Carbon taxes, 93
Carrying capacity, xii, 38, 84
Carson National Forest, 4
Carter Sand and Water Stop, 125

Catbrier, 119

Cattle, 131; as boom, 24–25; in Carson National Forest, 4–5; and ecosystem effects, 8; historic empires of, 50; and methane, 55; in Texas, 21–22, 124; and water, 47

Cedar brakes, 13

Central Valley, 44

CFC refrigerants, 38, 61. *See also* Ozone depletion

Champion International, vii, 125–126, 133

Changing Course, 84–85

Chicago, 47, 69, 121

Child labor, 44, 95–96

China, 38

Chlordane, 48

Chlorofluorocarbons. *See* CFC refrigerants

Civil War, 25, 108–109

Clean Water Act, 99

Clearcutting: and Big Thicket, xv, 26–27, 112, 114, 121, 126; and biodiversity, 54; and economic theory, 37, 75; as land modification, 12, 51. *See also* Monoculture; Tree farms

Climate change, 33–34, 54–56, 96. *See also* Global warming

Clinton-Gore administration, 89

CO₂. *See* Carbon dioxide

Coastal Zone, 22–24, 27, 100–101, 131–133

Cobb, C. W., 64, 67, 140

Colmesneil, 117

Cologne, Germany, 93

Colorado, xiii, 20, 44

Comal Springs, 46–47

Commons, the, 60, 74, 85

Concho River, 14

Connecticut, 121

Conroe, xv, 22, 117

Consequentialist ethics, 129

Corporate Average Fuel Economy, 97

Corpus Christi, 22, 73, 133

Correll, Donovan S., 111, 140

Corrigan, 125

Corsicana, 25

Cotton, 44; as boom, 24–25; ecosystem effects of, 14, 47, 49; and land use, 70; in Texas, 20–21

Cotton-mouth snake, 117, 119

Council of Economic Advisors, 66

Cranberry, 9

Cretaceous period, 53

Cypress swamps, xiii, 19–20, 118–120, 122–123

Dakotas, 24

Dalhart, xiii, 20, 27, 50

Dallas, 75; and ecology, 34, 52; and geography, 20; and population, 40, 131. *See also* Dallas–Fort Worth

Dallas County, 48, 62, 70

Dallas–Fort Worth, x, 22, 36, 40–41, 70, 127

Daly, Herman, 66, 68–70, 140

Dam B, 122

Dauerwald, 7

Davis Hill State Park, 123

DDT, 88

Deer, 1, 4–8, 10, 13, 90, 117, 121

Deontological ethics, 129

Department of Energy, 58

Devers, 125

Dillard Creek, 125

Diversity: aesthetic, 14; in Big Thicket, 110–111, 122, 127, 133; biological, 7, 15, 52–54; and frontier, xiv; and the land, xiii, 19–20, 23

Doucette, 114, 117–118

Dujay Sanctuary, 123

Dupont and Co., E. I., 59

Dust Bowl, 9, 14, 51–52

East Texas, vii, 111; and forestry, 71–72, 114; and forests, 12, 107; and water,

23, 45; and wetlands, 50. *See also* Woodlands

East Texas Railroad, 109

Eastex Corporation, 125

Eckhardt, Bob, 120

Ecological economics, xv, 72

Ecological footprint, xii, 41, 44, 52, 87, 135

Ecology, xi; and commerce, 89–94, 102–103; and frontier mythology, ix; and getting the price right, 96; as a land crisis, 83; and the land, 15; and land use, 98, 105, 127; laws of, 54; and Leopold, 35; as related to economics, xiv, 63–64, 75–76, 78, 107, 136; and Texans, 12; and water-use, 47, 99–100. *See also* Industrial ecology; Resource Conservation Ecology; Restoration ecology

Ecology of commerce, 89, 92–93, 102–103

Economic imperialism, 70–71

Economics, 100; and ecology, ix, xiv, xv, 94, 107; and ethics, 2; greening of, 82–83, 90; and history, 31; and land ethics, 63–66, 68–70, 72, 75–76, 78–79, 136; as theory, 61

Economic sufficiency, 73–74

Edge effects, 126

Edwards Aquifer, 46–47

Edwards Plateau, 21, 86. *See also* Hill Country

Ehrlich, Paul, 38, 91, 140

EIH. *See* Environmental Impact Hypothesis

Eisner, Thomas, 110, 140

El Paso, xiii, 20, 22, 34, 70, 74, 91

Endangered species, 31, 46, 82; and Big Thicket, 111; and development, 99; and economics, 66, 72, 76; and land use, 124, 127; and the market, 79; and Texas, 31, 52, 86, 132, 134; U.S. list of, xi

Energy, 10, 31–32, 44, 58, 64–66, 78, 82–84, 90–92, 96–98

Environmental aesthetics, 15. *See also* Beauty; Land ethics

Environmental Impact Hypothesis, xiv, 75–76, 142

Environmentalism, xii, xvi, 2, 33, 79, 110, 135–136

Environmental justice, 64, 139

Environmental law, xi, 87–88

Environmental management zones, 125

Environmental policy, 71, 88, 94

Environmental Protection Agency (EPA), xi, 48

Environmental regulation, 31, 76–78, 88

EPA, xi, 48

Ethics: types of, 16–17, 129. *See also* Land ethics; Land-reform ethics; Land-use ethics; Leopold, Aldo

Exotic plants, 49

Externalities, 69, 74

Extinction: and the American eagle, 88; mass, 52–53; rates of, 61; of the red-cockaded woodpecker, 12; and snowy egrets, 119; of species, 33, 44, 66, 73, 98; and water use, 46

Exxon Corporation, 89

Exxon Valdez, 89

Faulkner, William, 108

Federal Floodplain Insurance, 102, 124

Feeny, Paul, 110, 140

Ferns, 127

First World War, 24

Fish and Wildlife Service, 50

Fisheries, 27, 66, 86, 131, 133

Flader, Susan L., 7, 140–141

Fleas, 118–119

Florida Everglades, 110–111

Florida Keys, 20

Flowering plants, 53, 111

Ford, Gerald N., 122

Ford Plant, 93
Forest Service, 2–4, 6
Fowler Farm, 117–118
Foxes, 10
Frontier: and attitudes toward land use, 12; and the economy, 94, 97; experience of, 24–25; and the nation, 3, 120; and the original Texan, 32; and Texas, ix, xii–xiv, 19, 107, 130–133
Frontier mentality, ix, xiv, xvi, 12, 24
Frontier mythology, ix, 97, 105

Gallinules, 119
Galveston, 22, 27, 40, 73, 89, 133
Galveston Bay, xiv, 48–49, 66, 131, 135
Galveston Island, 25, 57
Game management, 6–7
Game Management (Leopold), 7, 98, 141
Gasoline tax, 88, 97
Geese, 10
Germany, 6, 7, 92–94
Getting the price right, xv, 88, 94, 96, 105
Giant Slurbs: as bioregion, 21–24; defined, xiv; growth projections, 40, 42–43, 84, 131; and habitat modification, 52, 99; and sustainable development, 87; and water, 35, 45–46. *See also* Texas Triangle
Gila Wilderness, 4. *See also* Wilderness
Global warming, 34, 56–57, 135–136
GNP, 64
Golden-cheeked warbler, 12, 86
Goldfarb, William, 99–100, 141
Goodbye to a River (Graves), 34, 41, 141
Grapes of Wrath (Steinbeck), 51
Grapevines, 10
Grasslands, 5, 13, 50–51
Graves, John, 34, 41, 49, 120, 141
Great Depression, 26, 64
Great Frontier, The, (Webb), 25, 32, 144
Great horned owl, 119

Great Lakes, 23
Great Plains, 50–51
Greenbelts, 82, 102, 127
Green economy, 84–86, 89–90, 92, 94
Greenhouse effect, 54–55
Greenhouse gases, x, 54, 56, 64, 96
Grimes County, 121, 125
Gross Domestic Product, 61
Gross National Product, 64
Groundwater, xiv, 45–47, 51–52, 82, 99–100
Groundwater overdraft, 47, 51
Grubbs Vocational College, 26
Guadalupe Mountains, 135
Guadalupe Mountains National Park, 22
Gulf of Mexico, 52, 65, 102, 108, 113, 124
Gunter, Pete A. Y., 12, 112, 140–141

Habitat fragmentation, 134
Habitat modification, xii, xiv, 37, 39, 49, 52
Hardin, Garrett, 60, 65, 141
Harvard University, 25
Hawaii, 15, 77
Hawken, Paul, 89–92, 141
Heard Nature Sanctuary, 104
Herbicides, 114
High Plains: 20–21, 24–28, 46–47, 50–52, 65, 68, 70, 131–133. *See also* Panhandle
Highways, 26, 43, 99, 112. *See also* Roads
Hill Country, 12, 21, 23, 46, 127
Holly, 115
Houston, 47, 69, 91; and geography, x, 22, 27, 133; and Gulf of Mexico, 113; and pollution, 75
Houston County, 125
Hunt, Lamar, 10
Hunting, xiii, 2, 4, 6–7, 26, 104, 108, 129

Huntsville, 108, 142
Hurricanes, 133
Hydrologic cycle, 69

In a Narrow Grave (McMurtry), 25, 142
Index of Sustainable Economic Welfare
    (ISEW), 66
India, 44, 64, 88
Indiana, 21
Indian massacre site, 125
Individualism, 25
Industrial civilization, 58, 129
Industrial ecology, 57, 78, 90
Insecticides, 89, 114, 135
Integrity: and beauty, 14; and Big
    Thicket, 109, 121; as criterion for
    judgment, 35–36; definition of,
    11–13; and ecology, xii; and eco-
    nomics, 105; of ecosystems, 96–97;
    and global ecology, 86, 89; and key-
    stone species, 53; and land ethic,
    xiii, 15–17, 75; and planning, 98,
    101, 103; and practicality, 82; and
    stability, 13; and Texas tomorrow,
    133–134; of water resources, 44, 48
Intergovernmental Panel on Climate
    Change (IPCC), 55–57, 144
Interstate 45, xv, 121
Irrigated agriculture, 28, 46, 131, 133
ISEW, 66
Ivory-billed woodpecker, 134

Jack Gore Unit, 122
Juneberry, 9
Jungle, 111, 115

Kansas, 9, 24–25, 44, 46
Kirby Enterprises, 125

Laguna Madre, 133
Lamar Technical College, 26
Lamar University, 111, 123
Lance Rosier Unit, 106, 122–123

Land-community ethics, 16–17
Land ethics: and Big Thicket, 49; and
    economics, xiv–xv, 32, 63, 75, 78–79;
    and the future, 135–136; as inspired
    by Leopold, 35; kinds of, 16–17; and
    the land community, xiii, 36; and
    other ethics, 129; and population,
    38, 41; practicality of, 81–82, 105;
    and sustainable development, 86;
    and Texas, xi–xii, 33–34; and Texas
    public policy, 94, 102; and waste, 57.
    See also Leopold, Aldo
Land-reform ethics, 16–17, 41, 58
Land-rights ethics, 16–17
Land-use decisions, 12, 69
Land-use ethics, 16–17, 57
Land-use planning, xv, 17, 94, 97–100,
    102–103, 105
Landfills, 48, 54, 57, 62, 100, 128. *See
    also* Solid wastes; Toxic waste dumps
Larson Sandyland Sanctuary, 123
Lavaca Bay, 48, 84, 88, 131, 133
Lawrenceville Prep, 2
Leopold, Aldo: archives, vii; in Big
    Thicket, 107, 114–120; and ecology,
    90; and economics, 69, 75; and the
    land, 133–134; and land ethics, xiii,
    1–11, 14–15, 17; and land-use plan-
    ning, 98, 102–103; and other ethics,
    129–130; and values, 35
Liberty County, 125
Lions, 70, 116
Live oak, 21
Livingston, 15
Loblolly pine, 109, 115, 117, 121
Loblolly Unit, 122
Longhorn cattle, 25
Longleaf pine, 109, 122, 125. *See also*
    Yellow pine
Los Angeles, 20
Louisiana, xv, 77–78, 108, 117, 121,
    125–126
Louisiana Pacific, 125–126

Louisiana Purchase, 108
Loving County, 22
Lumber companies, 3, 112, 121, 124–126. *See also* Champion International; Louisiana Pacific; Temple-Inland; Timber

McLeod, Claude A., 109, 112, 117, 121, 142
McMurtry, Larry, 25, 142
Magnolia Garden Club, 123
Mainstream economics, xiv, 64–65. *See also* Ecological economics
Mammals, xi, 10, 13, 52–54, 141
Man-made capital, 65–67. *See also* Natural capital
Manufacturing, 31, 64, 77, 83–85, 88, 93–94
Maquiladora industry, 48
Marginal utility, 68–69
Market, the: and beef, 46; and corporate behavior, 60, 82; and ecological consumer products, 93–96; and ecology, xv; and ecology of commerce, 89; and economic booms, 32; and environmental goals, 79; and getting the price right, 105; and incentives for recycling, 57; and land ethics, xii, 136; and land-use ethics, 17; and natural beauty, 14; nineteenth-century faith in, 3; and paper products, 44; and population growth, 41; and pricing natural resources, 69; and Texas, 132; theory of, 71–75; and timber, 114, 121. *See also* Ecology of commerce
Marketplace theory, 71, 73–75
Maryland, 21, 111, 121
Mass transit, 93–94, 98. *See also* Transportation
Matagorda Bay, 48, 131
Mayr, Ernst, 71, 142
Melbourne, 47

Menard Creek Corridor, 122
Mesquite, 13, 21, 107
Methyl mercury, 131
Mexico: and environmental problems, 87–88; and Texas geography, 20, 48. *See also* Gulf of Mexico; Rio Grande
Mexico City, 20
Meyer-MIT Study, 76–77, 142
Midwest, xiii, 11, 21
Migratory pathways, 99
Mining, 28, 31, 59, 71, 95
Minnesota, 101
Mississippi, 21, 24
Mississippi Delta, 108
Mississippi River, 2, 20
Monoculture, 44, 112, 114, 121. *See also* Clearcutting
Monsanto Plant, 58
Montana, 24
Montgomery County, 117
Moths, 13
Mountain lions, 70, 116
Multiplier effect, 40

Nannyberry, 9
National Aeronautics and Space Administration (NASA), 56
National Commission on the Environment, 61, 88, 97, 142
National forests, 3–6, 12, 122, 134
National Grasslands, 51
National Park Service Study, 110
Natural capital, 32, 52, 65–68, 71. *See also* Man-made capital
Naturalistic fallacy, 129
Nature's economy, 13, 64–65, 67–68, 102
Nebraska, 28, 46, 47
Neches Bottom Unit, 122
Neches River, 121–122, 125
Neutral ground, 108, 120
New Federalism, 77
New Mexico, 3–4, 6, 22, 77, 135

Nonpoint pollution, 87, 99
North Carolina, 44
North Sea, 58
Nuclear Regulatory Commission
    (NRC), 58
Nuclear wastes, 87–88

Oelschlaeger, Max, 79, 142–143
Ogallala Aquifer, xiv, 27, 46, 65, 70, 83,
    133
Oil: and Big Thicket, 49, 52, 107,
    109–110, 112, 124; as boom, 24–26,
    132; ecosystem effects of, xv, 12, 27,
    32, 74; import of, 97; as resource
    frontier, xiv
Omnibus Recycling Bill, 57
O'nyong nyong Fever, 39
Orchids, xv, 27, 111
Oregon, 77
Oriole, 13
Our Common Future, 85, 144
Overgrazing, 6, 8, 12, 50, 54. *See also*
    Cattle; Soil erosion
Overstory, 13, 111, 127
Oxygen, 72, 90
Ozone depletion, 33, 38–39, 60–61, 73,
    136

Padre Island National Seashore, 22
Palm trees, 22
Panhandle, xiv, 20–21, 83, 87, 89. *See*
    also High Plains
Pantex Plant, 57–58, 87–88. *See also*
    Nuclear wastes
Panthers, 1, 4–5
Paxton, P. J. ("Paxie"), 115–116
Perot, Ross, 65, 68
Petrochemical industry, 22, 24, 31, 38,
    66, 76, 89
Petrochemical plants, 16, 34, 48, 84, 86,
    88, 99–100
Piedmont, 110
Pileated woodpecker, 119

Pinchot, Gifford, 2–3, 6, 120, 122
Pine Island Bayou, 122–123
Pine trees, 26, 114–117, 119–126
Piney Woods, 12, 21, 24, 26, 131
Plum, 9
Plymouth Rock, 25
Pollution. *See* Air pollution; Insecti-
    cides; Nonpoint pollution; Water
    pollution
Population, xiv, 44, 63; attitudes to-
    ward, 82, 84, 100; and depopulation
    of High Plains, 28; and disease, 39;
    and economics, 64, 67, 69–70; eco-
    logical footprint of, xii, 45; ecosys-
    tem effects of, 60–61; and "feed-
    back," 91; and global warming,
    56–57; nonhuman, 4–5, 7–8, 72, 90,
    99, 104, 121, 124; projections of
    Texas growth in, 42–43; and sustain-
    able development, 87; of Texas, x–xi,
    35–38, 40–41, 132; and Trans-Pecos,
    58; and water, 45, 52
Population Bomb, The (Ehrlich), 91, 140
Post Oak Belt, 12, 21. *See also* Wood-
    lands
Prairie Country, 21, 23
Prairie of Texas, x–xi, xiv, 8, 21–24,
    35–38, 40–41, 74, 108, 110, 132; and
    beauty, 14; in the Coastal Zone, 27,
    125; ecosystems of, 49–51; educa-
    tional use of, 104; influence of de-
    velopment on, 70, 87, 131; and Leo-
    pold, 111. *See also* Grasslands
Precambrian, 20
Precautionary principle, 56, 89, 100
Predator extermination, 5
Principle of thirds, 102
Private property, 31, 94, 97
Puritans, 25

Quail, 33, 117

Railroads, 43–44, 109–110
Rainfall, 21, 45, 57, 72, 109, 136
Rainforests, 39, 44, 53–54, 56, 96
Raspberry, 7, 9
Rattlesnakes, 70
Razorbacks, 118
Reagan era, 77, 89
Recycling, 44, 57, 93
Red-cockaded woodpecker, 12, 134
Red River, 35, 84, 101, 104
Reptiles, xi, 13, 52–54
Resource Conservation Ecology, 2–3,
    120. *See also* Mainstream economics
Restoration ecology, 11
Reynolds, "Hacksaw," 93
Richards, Ann, 46
*Rio Declaration on Environment and
    Development*, 85–86, 89. *See also
    Agenda 21*
Rio Grande, 21–22, 48, 87, 89, 127
Rita Blanca Grasslands, 51
Roads, x, 43–44, 65, 98–99. *See also*
    Highways
Rockport, 133, 135
Rocky Mountains, 22
Rogers, Will, 101
Roosevelt, Theodore ("Teddy"), 2–4, 6
Rwanda, 38

Sabine River, 108, 117, 121
Safe Water Drinking Act, x
Sagoff, Mark, 78, 143
St. Regis, 125
Sam Houston National Forest, 122
San Antonio: and geography, x, 20, 22,
    131; and Giant Slurbs, 35, 40, 84;
    and water, 46, 86
Sand budget, 27, 100. *See also* Barrier
    Islands
Sand County Almanac (Leopold), 1, 9,
    35, 139, 141
Sand flies, 115
San Francisco, 25

San Marcos Springs, 86
Saratoga, 109, 114, 122, 126
Saudi Arabia, 44
Schmidheiny, Stephan, 84, 92, 143
Scrappin Valley, 125
Sea level rise, 27, 55–57, 144. *See also*
    Greenhouse effect)
Seymour, 135
Shortleaf pine, 109, 122
Sierra Club, 46, 84
Slurbs. *See* Giant Slurbs
Smith, Adam, 95
Snowy egrets, 119
Socrates, 60
Soil erosion, 37, 44, 51, 58, 61, 66,
    82–83. *See also* Topsoil
Soil types, 20
Solar energy, 90–91, 96
Solid wastes, 91
Somervell County, 49
Sour Lake, 109
South America, 44
Southern pine bark beetle, 114
Southern Pine Manufacturers Associa-
    tion, 120
Southland Corporation, 125
Spanish land lines, 115
Spanish moss, 19
Spearing, Darwin, 20, 143
Special Places in the Woods Program,
    125
Species, xiv; in Big Thicket, 111–112,
    114, 116, 124–125, 127, 133; and bio-
    system services, 72–73; and ecologi-
    cal footprint, 44–45; and economics,
    76, 79; extinct, 134; and habitat
    modification, 39; human, 13, 53, 91;
    and integrity, 12–13; keystone, 53;
    and Leopold, 2, 7–8, 10; and public
    policy, 82, 86, 98–99, 103–104; in
    Somervell County, 49; in Texas, xi,
    53–54. *See also* Biodiversity; Endan-
    gered species; Species extinction

Species extinction, 33, 66, 98
Spillover effects, 96
Spina bifida, 48
Spindletop, 25, 109
Squirrel, 119
Stability, 8, 16; and Big Thicket, 127; as
    criterion for judgment, 15, 17,
    35–36, 130; defined, 13–14; and
    economics, 75, 82; of global ecosys-
    tem, 32; in land ethics, xiii, 11; and
    public policy, 94, 98, 101, 103, 105;
    and Texas tomorrow, 133–134
Stanford University, 38
Steinbeck, John, 51
Stewart Hotel, 118
Stream channelization, 54
Substitutability function, 65. *See also*
    Mainstream economics
Superfund Law, xi, 32, 59. *See also*
    Toxic waste dumps
Suspended particulates, 114
Sustainability, ix, xi, xiv, 69, 131
Sustainable development, xiv, 84–85.
    See also Agenda 21
Swamp chestnut oak, 117
Swamps, xiii, xv, 20, 108, 117, 119–123
Symbiosis, 91

Take back program, 93. *See also* Recy-
    cling
Tamarisk, 13
Tamaulipas, 110
Tampico, 20
Taxes, x, 9, 40, 93, 102, 124
Temple-Eastex, 123
Temple-Inland, vii, 123, 125–126
Texas Agricultural and Industrial Col-
    lege, 26
Texas Books in Review, 120, 140
Texas General Land Office, 101
Texas Legislature, 12, 38, 47, 57
Texas Natural Resources Conservation
    Commission, 47, 84

Texas State Parks and Wildlife Depart-
    ment, vii, 123, 133
Texas Technological College, 26
Texas Triangle, x
Three Mile Island, 58
Throughput, 73
Tiger, 90
Timber: and Big Thicket, 114–115, 117,
    119, 122, 124; as boom, 25; and eco-
    logical footprint, 41, 131; frontier
    outlook on, 3; and land use, 49, 52;
    and Leopold, 4; as natural capital,
    32, 65–66; as product, 24; and regu-
    lation, 78; and T. Roosevelt, 3
TNRCC, 47, 84
Tokyo, 39, 47, 69
Tolar, 115
Topsoil, 14, 51–52, 66, 68. *See also* Soil
    erosion
Toxic chemicals, 33, 57–59, 87
Toxic waste dumps, 16, 59, 74
Toxic waste regulation, 59
"Tragedy of the Commons" (Hardin),
    60, 141
Trans-Pecos, 22–24, 58, 88
Transportation: alternative forms of,
    94, 97; and greenhouse gases, 64, 74,
    96; network, 43–44; of oil, 25; and
    population, 131; practicality of pres-
    ent system of, 83–84; private, xi; as
    social infrastructure, 78
Tree farms, 7, 44, 121. *See also* Clearcut-
    ting; Monoculture
Trinity Aquifer, 70
Trinity County, 125
Trinity River, 48, 101, 121–123, 127
Trinity River National Wildlife Refuge,
    123
TU Electric, 58, 141
Tupelo, xv, 20, 122
Turkey, 122
Tyler County, 125

U.S. Fish and Wildlife Service, 50
U.S. Forest Service, 2–4, 6
UNCED (UN Conference on Environment and Development), 84, 90. *See also Agenda 21*
Underground water, xiv, 21, 26, 28, 70, 99, 132–133. *See also* Aquifers
Understory, 13, 111, 115, 127
UNEP (United Nations Environment Program), 56
Union Carbide, 88
Union of Concerned Scientists, 74, 97
University of Texas, 17, 26; at Arlington, 26
University of Wisconsin, vii, 7, 9
Utah, 77

Valley View, 135
Vera Cruz, 110
Victoria, 22, 74
Village Creek, 115, 123
Volume tables, 115

Walker County, 125
Waste, xiv, 44, 65, 98; in ecology of commerce, 90–92; hazardous, 33, 48; and industrial ecology, 78; and Leopold, 10; municipal, 16, 92; radioactive, 87–88; site photograph, 30, 80, 128; and the state of neglect, 37–38; in Texas, 57–60, 74; in water, 48, 87
Water, 5, 37, 50; and beauty, 14–15; and Big Thicket, 49, 109, 117, 119–120, 125–126; and biosystem services, 60; crisis, 32–33; and ecology, 5–6, 13–14, 27–28; and economics, 61–72, 74, 95–96; and erosion, 51; and flooding, 43; frontier outlook on, xii, 3; and High Plains, 26; human dependence on, 8; lake, 12; and land ethics, 1, 76; and land-reform ethics, 16; overdraft, xiv; overuse of,

54; and public policy, 82–83, 86, 88–89, 98–100, 102, 104; in resource conservation ecology, 2; rights, 31; and Slurbs, xiv; and the state of neglect, 44–49, 78; and Texas geography, 20, 22–23; and Texas tomorrow, 131–133, 136; and urban supply, 34–36, 38, 41, 52. *See also* Underground water
Water pollution, x, 48, 54, 58–59, 66–67, 72, 82
Watersheds, 4, 6, 8, 36, 41
Water supply, 33, 38, 45, 47, 83
Water turkeys, 119
Watson, Geraldine, 111
Wealth of Nations (Smith), 95
Webb, Walter Prescott, 25, 32, 144
Welder Wildlife Refuge, 104
Wetlands: and Big Thicket, 125; destruction of, 50, 52, 54; and ecology, 33, 39, 96; and economics, 70–71, 76; effects of habitat fragmentation on, 12; and ISEW, 66–67; and Leopold, 10; and public policy, 82, 99–100; as source of methane, 55. *See also* Bottomlands; Swamps
Wheat, 10, 32–33
White oak, 117
Wichita, 46
Wild Azalea Canyons, 125
Wilderness: and Big Thicket, 108, 114, 126–127; and economic imperialism, 71; experience of, 24, 124; and ISEW, 67; and Leopold, 4, 9; and public policy, 78–79, 97–98, 102–103; and timber industry, xv–xvi
Wilderness Society, 9
Wild hogs, 124
Wildlife: and ecology, 12; and ecology of commerce, 92; and edge effects, 126; and Leopold, 7, 9; and public policy, 78; refuge for, xv, 22

Wildlife Society, 9
Wilfred Turner Nature Sanctuary, 123
Wilson, E. O., 52, 89
Wisconsin, vii, 6–7, 9–10
Wisconsin Conservation Commission, 9
Wisconsin River, 10
Wolves, 1, 4–5, 70, 134
Woodlands, 33, 49, 54, 109–110
Woodlands Region, 21–23, 25–26, 71, 107, 133
Woodville, 118

World Bank, 44
World War II: postwar development, 33, 46, 49, 51, 55, 70, 100, 131; postwar population growth, x, 35, 40
Worms, 50
Wyoming, 20, 44

Yale University, 2
Yarborough, Ralph W., 122
Yellow pine, 116
Yucca, 110, 123